GO GIRL

To everyone who is willing to step out of their comfort zone to chase their dreams.

Go for it!

To my family and friends—you are the wind beneath my wings.

GO GIRL

An inspiring journey
from bronze to gold

Hardie Grant Books

achieve your dreams

unleash your power

Published in 2001
by Hardie Grant Books
12 Claremont Street
South Yarra VIC 3141
www.hardiegrant.com.au

National Library of Australia Cataloguing-in-Publication Data:
Cook, Natalie.
Go Girl: an inspiring journey from bronze to gold.
ISBN 1 740640 23 3.
1. Cook, Natalie . 2. Women volleyball players – Australia – Biography.
3. Olympic Games (27th, 2000: Sydney, N.S.W.)
I. Drane, Robert. II. Title.
158.1

Edited by Michele Sabto
Cover, text design and typesetting by David Marrone
Photos on front cover, inside front, and inside back courtesy of News Ltd.
Printed and bound in Australia by McPherson's Printing Group

Starlink–accelerating excellence.

Natalie Cook is the founder of the Starlink Foundation. Starlink aims to present
young athletes with the best possible opportunity to reach their potential and
follow their dreams by providing a mental and physical environment that
produces and nurtures athletic stars.

Contents

Acknowledgements

Some people come into our lives and quickly go.
Others stay a while and leave footprints on our heart
And we are never the same!

I have been blessed by having many wonderful people in my life. A special thanks to my family: Beverley, Brian and David (my number-one fan) Cook. My grandparents Clarice and Roy Chapman and the late Cooks, Les and Betty, who have all loved me unconditionally. Together we have shared the wins and the losses and they have always provided me with a safe haven to which to return. It is vital to have the support of your family and I have been so very lucky to have them by my side throughout the journey.

To my friends: there are too many to name them all, so at the risk of leaving some out I will not mention names, but you all know who you are. Thank you for sharing the ride with me and for your ongoing encouragement and support.

There are certain stages in life when we all need a little guiding, a little coaching. I have been very fortunate to have had some of the best school teachers (Corinda High, 1987–91) and the most amazing coaches. Special mention to Rodney McLeod and Marcus Ringet, my swimming coaches, Robert Bischof and Brian Van der Weide on the indoor volleyball front—and of course the amazing Steve (IB) Anderson. Without their belief and support my achievements to date would not have been possible.

And, of course, my amazing team…the Dreamachine: Kerri Pottharst, Steve Anderson, Phil Moreland and Kurek Ashley. We did it! We smiled in the face of adversity and gritted our teeth at times when we could have taken it easy. We implemented the plan to a tee and I want to thank you for your efforts, for putting your heart and soul into the dream and for playing full out. We have given meaning to the adage that there is a pot of gold at the end of the rainbow! The Dreamachine also includes our medical staff, who keep the finely-tuned machine (my body!) out on the sand everyday, and our sponsors, especially Speedo, Suncorp Metway, Grand United, Visy and Oakley. They did a fantastic job, as did our training partners (a big thanks to all the boys).

To all those who believed in my dreams, I can't begin to thank you enough for your support. And even to those who didn't believe, thank you for making me work so much harder to prove you wrong!

My hat goes off to Robert Drane, who agreed to write this book with me and was given such tight deadlines. He told me he could write 10,000 words a minute. And believe me, he needed to. Thanks Robert.

The following people kindly agreed to give permission to reproduce photos and I gratefully acknowledge their assistance: Brian Cook, Jeff Zadow, Peter Spann, Damien Searle and Map Magazine.

Enjoy the journey from Bronze in Atlanta to Gold in Sydney, and watch the colour start to change well before we stepped out onto the sand in Bondi!

Foreword ·

By Laurie Lawrence...

In 1996 two very talented bronzed Aussie Olympians arrived in Atlanta with a dream to be Olympic gold medallists. Beach volleyball was a new Olympic sport, and these girls were on a quest for its first gold medal.

They had all the ingredients required for Olympic Gold: international experience, fitness, skill, talent, strength, a coach who had prepared them well and had them highly motivated. They excelled on the practice courts and from pre-tournament training observations, looked likely gold medallists. However, these girls lacked one simple ingredient vital for success: self-belief, a simple belief that the Olympic gold medal was their destiny. They sought that belief from others. When they asked the great Herb Elliott's help, Herb took them under his wing and related how his coach Percy Cerutty programmed him for gold in the 1960 Rome Olympics.

I sat with them in Atlanta and listened to Herb as he related stories of how Percy had him walk in a quiet forest, or listen to music, to gather the mental strength that became a great emotional reservoir to draw on when he raced. He related how the hardships endured during training were necessary—nothing more than "a remorseless march towards the inevitable": Olympic Gold.

Belief is not something you find in a poem or something you can drink out of a bottle. It is deeper...something burnt into your inner soul that makes you totally independent. True champions don't need others as crutches for success. If you are dependent on others you will only have your jugular ripped out in the dog-eat-dog competition arena. The real key to success is self-belief and independence. All other things become tools, not crutches.

Any road to success will be paved with the stones of failure and disappointment. But to real champions, these failures and disappointments are merely obstacles put there to test them. I have read somewhere that "a champion gets up when he can't". History records how at the 1996 Atlanta Olympics Natalie Cook and Kerri Pottharst were beaten in the vital match that would have taken them through to the gold medal match. They were shattered, but were able to fight back for an Olympic bronze.

And so began their incredible journey. In this book, Natalie records this journey from Atlanta to Bondi, where they were not only able to draw strength from the home town but also feed off a new-found belief that they, like Herb, were on a "remorseless march towards the inevitable": Olympic Gold.

As you enjoy this book and the adventure that Natalie lived to get to this moment, learn the strategies that she is teaching you. Live them in your own life. Live your own golden adventure. And remember that she also had times when it seemed like it wasn't going to work out the way she wanted, yet she stuck it out and achieved one of her ultimate dreams. Understand that your success is waiting for you, and on the day that you most feel like quitting know in your heart that your success is just one day past that day.

You are a stonemason, looking at your life as a stone that needs to be sculpted until it is the way you want it. The key is to know that the beautiful sculpture is in there just waiting to come out for the world to admire. Enjoy the entire process of shaping your life.

I would like to take this opportunity to congratulate Natalie and Kerri for being true champions. You are my heroes!

Lisa Curry MBE OAM

Champion, noun. 1. one that excels all others. 2. defender of a cause, one who fights for another. 3. hero.

In everyday life we see champions. Some win the gold medal, many don't. You don't have to win the gold medal to be a champion.

Champion people are those who know what they want, know how to get it, work hard and depend on themselves to get the absolute best out of themselves every single day. Champion people also help others become champions, through their experiences, inspiration and motivation.

Like Natalie, I was watching the Olympics on TV as a 10-year old. My hero was Shane Gould, who won three gold medals in swimming at the Olympics in 1972. I said to myself "I want to go to the Olympics like her and hold the Kangaroo above my head".

Dreams start young and continue year after year, the desire getting stronger and stronger as you work harder and smarter. Natalie's dream started off like the dreams of many other kids. It finished with the ultimate prize, an Olympic gold medal.

I look forward to reading Natalie's book and learning what it took for her to accomplish the ultimate, so that I may learn more, and pass it onto the people with whom I come in contact.

Read, learn, apply, and enjoy. The best way to generate force is to increase acceleration. Work fast to be fast. Make every day count.

Gold found on Bondi

The famous—some say infamous—chant rippled loudly around the stadium, straight up the tunnel and through my body: "Aussie Aussie Aussie! *Oi Oi Oi!*". Ten thousand voices as one. All of a sudden I felt at home, yet also anxious and a little afraid. My body didn't quite know how to react. There was no precedent for this in my experience. We were beyond being intimidated by the crowd, because we had finally learned how to make them our own, to harness their energy. But this was the Olympic final, and there was a time when our opponents represented everything I feared on the beach volleyball court.

The blindingly bright, golden opening at the end of the tunnel was growing with each step. The smell of the salty sea air was getting stronger. The sand between my toes was becoming warmer. As the adrenalin that I once associated with the fear of losing surged even faster through my veins, I smiled. I felt how I imagine Rocky Balboa felt when he walked out to face that invincible Russian and everything he represented.

As we left the tunnel and entered the sand, we became more convinced than ever that this was our chance to steal the show. Stuff the silver. We were going for gold. "Ladies and gentlemen, please make welcome, from Australia…Natalie Cook and Kerri Pottharst!" The crowd stood and cheered as though we had already won! What they didn't know was that we felt as though we already had!

As we completed our warm-ups and sat down to wait for the start, Kerri and I looked into each others' eyes and clasped hands. I said "This is our opportunity. This is our stadium and this is exactly what we've worked so hard for. Let's enjoy the fight". We had been through a lot of learning, overcome a lot of barriers and I, in particular, had experienced many personal transformations in order to be here. For that, I was already grateful, regardless of the outcome. Yet, at the same time, I felt as though I was sitting for the final exam. What a tough test it was going to be! And I was determined to enjoy every moment.

We'd faced this pair fifteen times before, and we had won just once. But today we were convinced there was no history. The playing field was completely level. It was a brand new day in some ways. In other ways it was a day we had lived through so vividly so many times in our minds.

We faced our opponents off at each end line and ran into the net to shake hands and wish each other luck. Kerri took the ball to serve and the whistle signalled the beginning of the fight of our lives. The game started fast, with a tough, 82 km/h serve by Kerri that split the middle and gave us our first point. A dig in transition gave us a 2–0 lead. Although I was a little nervous, I settled once the leather slapped my forearms as I passed the first ball. At the first change of ends, we sat down and took in Bondi's carnival atmosphere. A Mexican wave travelled in slow motion around the arena. It was so dream-like that I had to pinch myself, but a thunderous roar snapped me out of my reverie as we walked back onto the court.

At 4–2, the score seemed to hover forever. Neither team seemed to be showing any sign of weakness, but something was bound to break. Suddenly, Brazil took the lead for the first time, at 6–5, went quickly to 7–5, then shot ahead to 8–5! The momentum was starting to tip in their favour. It seemed a small lapse of concentration on our part but, at this level, a tiny opportunity is all a team needs, and a three-point break in a

> Concentration is the ability to think about absolutely nothing when it is absolutely necessary.
>
> *Ray Knight*

The dig!

Kerri remembers the gold medal match

As far as I am concerned I have never been so focused, determined and prepared for any match. I played in an absolute cocoon of concentration: each point at a time, each with the same intensity. That was how I played my utter best. My level of awareness was consistent throughout: no big ups; no big downs. There was no crucial psychological turning point, or if there was, it wasn't until the last ball hit the sand: at that point the cocoon shattered and I collapsed to the sand.

game is considered an unassailable lead. In order to stop the bleeding, we called a time-out.

Not long after we resumed, something extraordinary happened that tipped the psychological balance our way and kept it there. It had such an effect on the outcome that, from that moment, it didn't matter what the scoreboard said. What happened was this: Adriana served, and her serve hit the top of the net and began its trickle over to our side and onto the sand. Of course, as soon as it hit the net, everyone in the stadium, including Kerri, thought it was going to ground—except me! For months I had been attempting to dig this very same ball in practice. We had decided that if this ever occurred, the setter would go for it, as she would be heading towards the net anyway, and only had to continue her momentum. However, in all the months we had practiced it, I had never touched such a ball, let alone dug one with any control.

I was already moving towards the net when the ball hit the top and began to drop. If I had ever doubted my ability to dig those balls, that doubt was now gone. "Go! Go! Go!" I told myself as the ball quickly made its decision to fall over our side. As it plunged, I took off. I felt as though everything was in slow motion. Although I'm sure the ball took less than a second to fall, it seemed to remain in the air as though controlled by an invisible wire. For that second, it was as if I was under water. I couldn't hear the clamour from the crowd, and my own voice filled the inside of my head.

And before I knew it, the world came rushing back in. I was on the sand, just as the ball got there. The crowd noise exploded again as though someone had suddenly flicked a switch. With one outstretched arm, I dug it high enough for Kerri to set magnificently to the corner. The Brazilians had no time to react—it all happened too quickly. If what I did was a surprise to Kerri, she sure didn't show it. She finished off as though we had successfully practiced the move a thousand times. It was a sideout (a handover of the ball to give you a chance

Flying high

to serve for a point), and the turning point of the match. I got up, and as I removed the sand from by body with a wry smile, I looked through the net at my opponent Shelda. The look of utter disbelief on her face fuelled my fire. I could tell that, at that point, she realised we couldn't be beaten. More importantly, so did I.

Once I had let go and realised that I was destined for gold, I decided to have a little fun with the crowd. I was in the zone and wanted to give the people an experience of a lifetime, to make them feel a huge part of our success. I was pumped, and every time we won a point I would turn to the crowd and throw my arms up encouraging them to roar louder. I could feel the adrenalin course through my body. I felt super-human. I wanted to deflate the Brazilians. For the first time ever they had to contend with a crowd that was not on their side. I knew this would have an impact beyond what the eye could see. I felt the energy, strength and excitement of 10,000. What a rush! It put a huge smile on my face, and allowed me to dig my heels in further, jump higher, run faster and feel stronger.

Soon after, we were down 11–8. To onlookers, it seemed as though we couldn't bridge that three-point margin. We'd been here before, many times, against Adriana and Shelda, and in the past, it would have been a sign of things to come. Adriana Behar and Shelda Bede were again everything we expected them to be: cunning, strategic, strong, talented. But this time, something had happened that made a difference. We found ourselves enjoying every moment of it! At that point in the match, we called a time-out. During that time, we quietly reminded ourselves of our goals, the first of which was to keep having fun. We were growing, and we could feel it. They were shrinking, and we could see it. If no one else could see it, it didn't matter. In our minds' eyes, we could see them undergoing a transformation. At 11–8 down, you could say it was a precarious time in the match for us. But that day it wasn't, because we chose not to see it that way.

Smiling, we marched back onto court, and Kerri served an ace. 11–9. A minute later, it was 11–10 as Adriana got called for a net touch. We were reeling them in! At 11–all, I went back to serve, knowing that this may be my only opportunity to close out the set. I looked up. Shelda had snuck over to the middle of the court, leaving me some room down her line. I threw the ball up, caught it with a slap to remove any excess grains of sand, brought it to my lips and kissed it for luck.

The whistle blew. I tossed it up, launched myself into the air and rolled my arm through, slicing the side of the ball with my hand to drag it over to the left. I watched it in what now seems like slow motion. It hit the top of the net, seeming to deliberate for a second over which way it should fall. Watching the ball teeter on top of the net was like waiting for Caesar's thumb to point up or down. What was the verdict to be? For once in this situation, it decided in my favour—the ball dribbled down their side of the net, and plopped onto the sand untouched. We had won the first set!

I had fate to thank for those two serves that changed the course of the match. In January, 2000, the sport's governing body, the Federation of International Volleyball (FIVB), had introduced a ruling that allowed play to continue after the ball had hit the net on serve. The players were generally opposed to this ruling. I recall a round-table discussion at which players said how terrible it would be if a gold medal match was won or lost like that. But a rule was a rule, and all we could do was accept it like the professionals we were, then develop strategies to turn it to our advantage in matches.

During a hard-fought, slugging second set, we again found ourselves behind on the scoreboard, and seemingly unable to haul in a two-point margin. But at 10–8, we could feel that surge about to unleash itself again. It was welling up inside us. Adriana and Shelda knew by now that a two-point lead wouldn't stop us rising to the occasion yet again. As the tension mounted, we could really sense that a shift had taken place. We could taste the win, and we were salivating! What's more, we could smell fear coming from the other side of the court. I'd never felt these sensations so strongly before, but then, our game had never *been* in this place before. Many people talk about 'the zone', but it's very rare to actually be in it. It's even rarer when it expands to envelop you and your partner.

Herb Elliott describes it as the relentless movement towards the inevitable. We marched toward that 12th and match point with so much desire and passion that no one could have stopped us on the day. We were on a mission. Blow by blow we matched the Brazilians, hitting back with combinations of power and finesse, making some great plays and converting them for points. As we continued to exchange service with them, the crowd was ecstatic. They were off their seats, standing on their seats, screaming, yelling, clapping. All the agony and ecstasy of four people on a volleyball court seemed to be multiplied tenfold in the reactions of the crowd. The final point was near, and everyone could feel it.

It came when one of our most powerful weapons—Kerri's serve—sliced between Adriana and her sideline for an ace. Suddenly, it was 11–10. Match point! Kerri went back to the service line. Could this be it? I was standing at the net calling her to serve the middle. She rifled one toward Shelda that caught her off guard and she passed it close to the net. As I jumped to block, Adriana got to the ball first with her knuckles and it sailed over the top of me. I knew that it would have been out. I turned to move towards the ball and saw Kerri flying through the air. My heart skipped a beat—I thought she might just touch it! But she left it and it landed wide. The linesman's flag went up and the ball was called out! And from that moment, we were called *Olympic champions!*

As the crowd rose, Kerri and I fell to the sand. I could hear, above the thunderous roar, the disjointed announcements over the PA: "Gold... Australia... Pottharst and Cook...Gold medal!"

It's a magical day when a mission is accomplished.

Part 1

Awakenings

Chapter 1

It all starts with a dream

When I was seven years old, I was sitting on the floor watching the 1982 Brisbane Commonwealth Games on the television when I saw Lisa Curry standing on a podium, receiving a gold medal around her neck for winning the 100 metres freestyle. I said "I want to do that!" At about the same age, I was watching the football on the television with my dad and a physiotherapist ran onto the field to help someone who was hurt. I said "I want to do that!" Believe it or not, those two simple realisations helped shape my life. They were my first real dreams. They are one of the reasons I won a gold medal at the Sydney Olympics; why I did two years of physiotherapy at the University of Queensland, before beach volleyball came along; and why I'm writing this book. I've come to know these things about myself: I like to win, an

It all starts with a dream.

> *Restlessness is discontent—and discontent is the first necessity of progress. Show me a thoroughly satisfied man—and I will show you a failure.*
>
> Thomas Edison

I also understand that I'm the sort of person who has to 'see' things before I decide I want to *do* them. Just as well there was such a thing as television back then! For a long time, I wanted to be like Lisa Curry, and like that physiotherapist. Having people such as these as heroes and role models acts as a kind of magnetism. You begin to attract things to yourself that those people have; things that help you to realise your dreams. Dreams are visions. We 'see' them and 'feel' them and think "Wow—that would be awesome. I wish I could have that!" Well, you can. It's only a matter of *really* wanting it.

> **The best and fastest way to learn…is to watch and imitate a champion.** *Jean-Claude Killy*

From the ages of seven to fourteen, I'd plough up and down pools, singing and reciting television commercials as I blew the bubbles out of my mouth and nose. I used to love competing in the carnivals. I reached the state level and represented Queensland at the National Titles.

At the age of fourteen, I realised that swimming wasn't for me, for many reasons. I would wake up at crazy hours of the morning to get to training, in the quest to be like Lisa. Mum had to make sure I didn't just throw the alarm through the window, roll over and go back to sleep. Basically, I got sick of that black line. Swimming up and down a pool didn't really satisfy my competitive urge, or give me the surge of adrenalin that I needed to be at my very best. But the vision of Lisa Curry has stayed with me forever. It was a vision of success, of being number one.

So I tried my hand at just about everything. I did martial arts, golf, tennis, even skateboarding. But they were all individual sports and, when I hit high school, I felt the need to be in a team sport for a change. The idea of being part of a team appealed to me.

I strongly believe that everything happens for a reason. One ordinary day, when I was fourteen and in year nine at Corinda High, I saw a notice on the board at school that said "volleyball trip to America and Canada". I walked upstairs and said to the teacher, "I'd love to go to America and Canada. What's volleyball?" The teacher took me down the hall to where the boys were playing and he said "that's volleyball". I said "Great! How do I play?" I still knew what I wanted to be—a champion—and the travel sounded exciting, so I learned to play volleyball.

I played at first with the boys because there wasn't a girls team. Games were played on a 'rotation' system. Whenever you made a mistake, you were off! Often, I was ordered off even when I hadn't touched the ball! The boys always agreed it was my fault! At first, I'd say "Yeah, whatever." and go off. But as my skills began to improve, I'd stand my ground and say "No! I was nowhere *near* the ball. It was *your* fault. *You* get off". I stayed on the court, and I continued to develop as a volleyball player.

To fund our trip we all had to work hard to raise money, car washing and selling raffle tickets. It was so gratifying to take all the right steps, see the improvement, and have the added bonus of fulfilling my dream to travel.

I felt a little more like a volleyballer after my trip, and not long after my return I was dragged along to Ipswich in Queensland by Carmen, a friend of mine, to try out for the regional schools volleyball team. And that's when I developed my first positive conception of what I could be as a volleyballer. I really hadn't played enough of the sport to believe I was good at it. But, because of my height, I caught the attention of the coach, Brian Van Der Weide. He simply said "I want you to jump up and hit the ball as hard as you can. I don't care where it goes. I don't care if it hits the back wall on the full. Just hit the thing as hard as you can". To this day, I can honestly say that that was the best hit I've ever done!

Thanks to Brian, I developed a potent weapon that has stayed with me. He could have worried about all sorts of technical details, but he encouraged me to *start with my strength*. More than that, he helped me to identify it. Many of us with low self-esteem do not hear encouraging words for what they are. But sometimes there are clues in there as to what our strengths are, so we should be all ears. It's not a lack of humility to take on board someone's praise.

Thanks to Brian I developed a vision of myself as being big and powerful. It doesn't matter if it's true or not. He held up a particular mirror to me. I looked in that mirror and saw someone who could win volleyball games. I needed that, and Brian was the right person at the right time, but only because I chose to believe him. And, deep down, most of us like to believe an encouraging word.

I fell in love with volleyball and went on to state and national junior sides, all the while doing something else I love to do: travel.

**Whatever the mind can conceive and believe,
the mind can achieve.**

Jean-Napoleon Hill

Chapter 2

Focus!

Back at school, during volleyball training sessions, I'd hear my coach chant a familiar refrain: "You're not focusing!" I didn't understand what he meant, and neither did any of the others. "What are we supposed to bloody focus on?", we asked each other. The goal was defined this way: pass the ball here, set the ball there, and hit it over there. And win. Easy enough to follow. But we didn't understand the mechanics of focusing. Were we supposed to focus on getting to the ball, or passing the ball, or moving our feet, or looking at the ball, or maybe on what parts of our anatomy were doing, like our shoulders or our arms? What component of the overall skill were we supposed to focus on?

A few of us decided to turn the word "focus" backwards and say (out of the coach's earshot) "sucof". It was safer than saying f*** off! By turning it into a joke, we would forget all the technical issues that were bogging us down and holding us back. And we would focus on the outcome, rather than on what he wanted us to focus on. Even then I realised that I personally had to have a clear vision of what I wanted the ball to do. A clear vision of the outcome. As my coach now says, the ball doesn't have a brain, so make it do what you want it to do.

These days, I focus on outcomes: the path of the ball and where it will end up. That is, where *I want it to end up*. When my mind sees that, all my other actions adjust themselves accordingly. It was an important step toward understanding myself, and the way I process information. It was also an important pointer to what I should do in life. All my actions would either lead me away from, or toward, where I want to end up, not only sports-wise, but as a human being. The desire to see outcomes was not a fault—it was one of my strengths. The outcome was something for me to *focus* on.

At the time I was still trying a lot of different sports, despite my initial success at volleyball. But there came a huge turning point in September of 1993. I was 18 and a member of the Queensland senior team competing in the National Grand Prix in Brisbane. I was probably considered one of the best junior volleyballers in Australia. Not long after Sydney was announced as the venue for the 2000 Olympic Games, it was also announced that beach volleyball was to become an Olympic sport. Prior to this, beach volleyball was considered a "fun", summer version of the indoor variety of the game. All volleyballers played indoor seriously, and ventured out onto the beach for a tan. Since its inception in Australia, Anita Palm and Jacqui Vukosa were our number one team, and had travelled offshore to represent Australia. Anita approached me one day and asked, "would you like to move to Sydney and train with me full time and go to the Atlanta Olympics?"

I told her I needed a few days to think about it. But in the week that followed, I felt empty. Something just wasn't right. I awoke one morning, rolled out of bed and kicked myself. I was denying myself the very opportunity I'd dreamt about! I quickly dialled Anita's number. Thankfully, she was there to answer! I asked, "Is the offer still open? I can be on the next plane. Let's go to the Olympics!"

So I stepped on a plane and left behind my family, friends, and the physiotherapy degree to chase my dream. There were no guarantees—only opportunities.

> **We are what we repeatedly do. Excellence, then, is not an act, but a habit.**
>
> *Aristotle*

Remember this

- Having a dream is vital. We all need something to aspire to.
- We can learn a lot by observing how the best do things.
- Encouragement has a nourishing effect, especially when we choose to hear the good words and reject—or learn from—the bad.
- Knowing our strengths is a great place to start!
- A vision of the future is an excellent focal point. If we're not sure what that vision is, we should make it clearer, until it comes into sharp focus.

Chapter 3

Atlanta

Physiotherapy was put on hold, and has been there ever since. I don't know that I'll ever return to it, but I learned a lot about physiology and how systems work, and have maintained that interest, in various ways, ever since.

In 1995, Anita and I decided to go our separate ways. I teamed up with Kerri Pottharst, one of our best-ever indoor volleyballers, who took up beach volleyball to prolong her career (after a bad knee injury). In August 1995, we made a breakthrough: in Portugal, we had our first top-four finish on the world tour. It was an eye-opener because, for the first time, we realised that, as a team, we might just have what it took. But we needed a coach. We literally flew straight to the shores of California, in search of the next piece in the puzzle. We interviewed about six coaches, telling them they had two hours to teach us everything they knew about the sport. By the time we left to come home, we had chosen Steve Anderson, who impressed us with his approach to the game and his teaching methods.

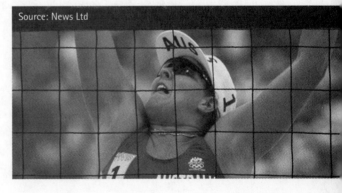

Source: News Ltd

We immediately began to make an impact. By the end of 1995, we were number one on the Australian circuit, and were giving a few international sides quite a shake. The Olympic dream was looking good. We easily gained selection for the Games in early 1996, and we just couldn't wait to get there. Everyone back home was excited by our opportunity to represent Australia, and we were surrounded by encouraging and loving friends and family. Everything seemed to be falling into place. We had had a dream run, and experienced little adversity, even though we were yet to win an international tournament. At least we had beaten some of the world's best teams along the way.

Atlanta came around quickly. At the age of 21, I was barely prepared for the intensity and the incredible sense of occasion. Here we were, exponents of a new sport at the Games, and rubbing shoulders with Kieren Perkins, Sam Riley, Susie O'Neill, and the Awesome Foursome. It was inspiring to hear people such as the great Herb Elliott and Laurie Lawrence address the team. At the time, as they talked about fear, doubt, pressure, hunger, as well as personal growth through hardship, obstacles, difficulties, and challenges, I thought I understood exactly what they meant. But as I said, I was yet to experience any real adversity.

> **Do not fear the winds of adversity. Remember, the kite rises against it rather than with it**

They advised us to *welcome* adversity, and uncertainty, and to thrive on them. They then told us to ask ourselves: "Why am I here?" I remember writing in my Atlanta diary, "I am here to win! Nothing less will cut it. 'If you act the part, eventually you will become it".

All through our preparation for Atlanta, my self-talk was so positive. By the time we arrived, I was pumped and excited to be there. It all sounded so right at the time, and I felt I was on the right track. Here is a collection of quotes I wrote in my diary just before the Games began:

Don't let you fears control your dreams—NO FEAR.

The greatest mistake one can make is to be afraid of making one.

Success is not a destination...it's a journey.

Teamwork is the ability to work together towards a common vision. It is the fuel that allows common people to attain uncommon results.

The harder you work the luckier you get.

Whether you think you can or think you can't, you're right.

Steve Anderson on fear

The fear doesn't really go away. It's what you do with it that counts. And that's what we do in competition. It doesn't get easier. You have to become more comfortable with fear, and facing it might get simpler, but it doesn't get easier.

" **It's what you learn after you know it all that counts** "

It all sounds so right, doesn't it? And it is. But deep down, I'd begun to develop a powerful sense that something was missing, and I just couldn't figure out what it was. In hindsight, all the positive self-talk was just surface chatter. My heart didn't buy into any of it.

I just didn't realise at the time that what I'd done very well was grasp the theory. What I probably needed to understand better was that the learning we do is only *true* learning when it's *implemented*. And that meant I still had to *experience*, first hand, a lot of the 'fear, doubt, pressure, hunger, hardship, obstacles, difficulties and challenges' that Herb and Laurie told us about.

There's a telling entry in my diary back then, in amongst all the positive stuff. It was just before we entered the Olympic Village when I wrote: "physically not working too hard but the mind is working overtime to stay positive". I then went on to write how I *deserve* to win gold, and that this was our opportunity to execute, execute, execute! But that little emotional detour revealed a lot about where I was really at. I thought that, if I could keep *telling* myself I was motivated, it would come.

Coming into the Games, I was scared. There's no doubt about it. I was letting little things get to me, as though I was internally making excuses before I'd even begun! Even then, I told myself that frustration is no solution, but fear and doubt were different matters. One day I was so down at training, and it affected my performance so much, that Kerri and Steve came down pretty heavily on me. And it was all because I was hanging on to one thought: "What if I fail?" I probably didn't know it but, somewhere in the depths of my mind, succeeding meant not failing—because failing is what I was really afraid of. The line between success and failure is so fine that we rarely know when we pass it; so fine that we are often on the line and don't even know it. I had my toe on that line!

Beach volleyball is a tough game, and your destiny rests heavily on the shoulders of your team mate. One day, after a practice, Kerri stuck a note on our door. It said "The way we play as a team determines success…we may be two great players, but if we don't play together, we're not worth a cent". At the time,

I thought Kerri looked despondent at training. I thought she was giving up, and I was getting angry. I realise now how much these things are a 'loop'. Who knows who it really starts with? She was probably as affected by my attitude as I was by hers. She probably even detected my doubts.

We were getting aggressive toward each other on the court during practice: "Stop being a bitch". "Shut up and look interested". We were no longer playing our opponents. We were playing each other. We resolved our differences, and continued in our determination to slay the opposition. But these ups and downs were telling behaviour. At one point I wrote, "It's scary to think that the confidence comes and goes like that. I hope it's there on the day". Doubts were beginning to creep in. I was *trying* so hard. The Voice that I brought with me everywhere kept having the last say, but I was yet to understand its power. The Voice was saying "You suck" and "You're not good enough", and I was trying hard to have it say something else, or to create an alternative voice to answer it. It was actually my biggest opponent. I was beginning to become aware of its ability to sabotage my performance. I just wish at that point I had a way to control it. We just might have had another gold medal.

I'm so pleased that I recorded my thoughts in my diary. The good thing about keeping a diary is that it is a terrific aid to self-reflection. Self-awareness is the starting point to eliminating negative emotions, and writing down what you really feel—knowing that no one will read it unless you want them to—is a very good way to begin reflecting on your own behaviour. The diary is like a 'third party', much like a counsellor or a therapist. It can't judge you or hold any expectations.

However, it was another 'third party', team psychologist Mark Spargo, who managed to weasle out of me my true feelings: fear of not reaching my expectations; of not playing well; of failing. It was the first time I'd articulated them to another person, and I did it after the opening ceremony and before our first match! I was hoping like hell that all the extra emotion and adrenalin would give me 'the eye of the tiger'. But you can't really get your energy from emotion, because emotion, on its own, is such a fickle thing.

Remember this

- Life has doubt and uncertainty. We can't make it more predictable—but we can develop the behavioural flexibility to deal with it successfully.
- Unless learning is implemented, it's just theory.
- Any aid to self-reflection is important if you want to address who you are, and who you want to be. It might be a friend, a counsellor, or a diary. A 'third party' is a big help.
- Don't rely on your emotional state for energy. You gain energy from the way you choose to perceive, and react to, circumstances.

Chapter 4

The Games begin!

I'd put myself through a thousand deaths before we finally got to the first game in Atlanta, against the English team of Cooper and Glover, but we had a great game plan, and it ultimately got us through those first-round nerves. We won relatively easily, 15–4. Our four-point plan went pretty well: 1. Make them small. 2. Serve aggressively. 3. Target Audrey. 4. Finish strong. Pretty simple really, but we liked the KISS (Keep it simple, stupid) theory. With a complicated game plan you can be bogged down in too much paralysing detail.

The next day, we hammered the American team of Gail Castro and Deb Richardson, 15–2, and felt vindicated, as they were seeded where *we* should have been, due to a ruling by the international body. We used that little annoyance as our motivation, and played strong, error-free volleyball. They were so excited to be at the Games that they didn't know what hit them when they found themselves in front of a home crowd of 11,000. The match also taught us a little about playing in front of huge, vocal home crowds, and we filed that one away for Sydney!

The win put us exactly where we wanted to be: a showdown with Reno and McPeak. Now, to put this in perspective: Reno and McPeak had dominated the 1996 season, winning six out of eight events leading into Atlanta. They were an awesome combination, but had experienced some teamwork issues as the Games drew closer. Everyone began to see a weakness in their armour. Kerri and I had done our homework, and we were ready to play them.

Our game plan was perfect. We had Holly in trouble from the very first serve, and played some awesome volleyball that put them under a lot of pressure before we even realised that we'd jumped out to a 13–8 lead. The game seemed to move so quickly, but you can never rest on your laurels, and the Americans pegged us back to 13–12, after Reno got fired up in a (non-verbal—all body language) exchange with me. It was like two tigers in a cage! But we managed to withstand the surge and won the match 15–13. It felt like a great triumph. We had not just overcome a great team, but we put ourselves exactly where we needed to be. The big crowd was parochial, chanting "USA, USA", the whole time. But we decided to hear it differently, and in our minds it became "AUS!" We came through, so it was a great psychological boost, especially after we saw the look on the faces of our opponents after the match! We never wanted to feel that way.

This put us into the semi-final against Monica Rodrigues and Adriana Samuel—the second Brazilian team—for a place in the no-lose medal final. We would get at least a silver if we won this match, but if we lost, we could have ended up fourth—an athlete's worst nightmare. All that hard work to get so close to the medals—yet so very far!

It was at this point that my fears finally kicked in. All the bandaids started to peel away. No amount of positive self-talk would pull me out of this one. My heart just didn't believe any of it, and the lead-up to this match was the worst possible time to realise this. Throughout the game, I focused on *not losing*, instead of on winning. They were always a scary team for me, and all through our 15–3 loss, my Voice kept telling me that I wasn't good enough to win. It kept asking questions like "What if it doesn't go to plan? What if we lose?"

We had won all of our games right through to the semi-final, and along the way we had defeated the number-one team, from the USA. Yet, when we got to that semi-final, doubts that I didn't even know I had came to the surface. So I

Jump serving in Atlanta

suppose, in retrospect, it shouldn't surprise me that at 3–2 down we thought it was all over! Correction: *I* felt it was all over. I felt as though I was at the bottom of a mountain, looking up. It looked way too hard to come back. At this point, I felt that I wasn't good enough. I felt unfit, slow, and lacking in mental strength. I had found a lot of reasons why I couldn't win. We always seem to find those voices very readily. I just couldn't hold on to a positive attitude any longer. I felt nervous and under-prepared. I had my Voice saying "This team's too good today, Nat". There was nothing on the other side to balance that Voice. From then, it was a downward spiral. The harder we tried, the worse it got, and I began to feel helpless, as though it was all out of my control. The positive self-talk was nowhere to be heard. It hadn't even shown up on the day!

Physically, Kerri and I were capable of winning a gold medal in Atlanta, but not mentally and emotionally. The fact is that, at this elite level of

Steve on the Atlanta opposition

Our skills were not as good as the Americans and Brazilians, passing, setting and just the basic skills. America and Brazil produce sportspeople with exceptional skills. They are very strict with their rules, the history and everything else. Since then our ball control has really developed, to the point where we are on a par with those teams with so much history and culture of ball control.

beach volleyball, everybody's skills are about equal. Everyone can hit, pass, set, and serve the ball. It all comes down to the mind of the athlete. Kerri and I hadn't been in a winning position enough as a team to believe or understand that we could do it. What's more important, we hadn't run our minds, our bodies, our nervous systems, through the experience of winning.

It took a loss to realise we had a lot of fight in us, and we decided we weren't going to leave without a medal. As I wrote in my diary, "Learnt a lesson today *but* not a good time to have to learn it!"

" A champion is someone who gets up when they can't. "

Chapter 5

Confidence tricks

Back in 1996, if you'd spoken to anyone who knows me, they'd have said I was never short on self-confidence. I had a belief in my ability, but I didn't know *what it meant to really believe in myself.* My self-belief was all superficial, and soon cracked under certain types of pressure.

I later realised the pressure was not actually external. It didn't come from opponents. They were just people playing to the best of their ability. It came from within. In other words, it was a pressure I was putting on myself. Therefore, it was unnecessary, and it could be changed only by one person: Natalie Cook. If I blamed anyone else, I was just avoiding the problem. If I was in awe of those opponents who I believed were putting the pressure on me, I was giving them more power than they deserved.

I'd already been there once, when I was a kid, and wanted to be a champion swimmer. But I kept losing to a girl who was half my size. I would say to myself, "She's too good; she's too quick. I can't do it". One day, for some reason, I changed it. I started saying "I'm too big to let her beat me". I didn't lose to her again from that day on. It was a change in my self-talk; a change in the way I viewed myself and my ability. There was not one physical change. It was all in my mind.

It took two years after Atlanta before my beliefs actually began to etch themselves into my heart and mind. At first, it was very hard. I had an emotional block about hollow "motivational" techniques, and

> **It's lack of faith that makes people afraid of meeting challenges, and I believed in myself.**
>
> *The Greatest—Muhammad Ali, who lit the flame in Atlanta*

GME

Gold

belief

attitude   focus   consistency

balance   fun

medical   training & hard work   sponsors

desire   preparation   team   discipline

DREAM   turn bronze into gold

Working from the top down. Each block is as important as the next. Without the right foundation, the block will not sit right

when I later came across the real thing, I didn't recognise it at first. It takes a lot of understanding to tap into real motivation and belief.

The difference between the Atlanta Games and Sydney was that, in planning for Sydney, Kerri and I sat down and said "Okay. Gold is the target. How do we make it happen?" We had specifically defined the goal, and we knew that taking the Holy Grail was entirely up to us. We would now work backwards from the gold. And the brain would tell the body exactly what it needed to do to achieve that. Somebody once asked Jimi Hendrix what made him a great guitarist. He said he didn't focus on the individual notes. He concentrated on the entire passage, and his fingers would rapidly do the rest. We began to focus on outcomes, something not taught by psychologists who insist that, if you focus on the process, the results will come. Sydney was still a long way into the future, but this shift in our thinking was an important starting point for us.

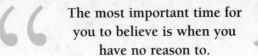

> **The most important time for you to believe is when you have no reason to.**

By the time we got to Sydney, Kerri and I were mentally and emotionally able to put ourselves on the top first, even before stepping out on the sand. From there, all the steps we needed to take were far clearer, and it sure is a better view from the top of the mountain than it is from the bottom! But, as I said, Sydney was still a long way into future, and this book is all about how we got there. In Atlanta, we were still standing at the bottom, hoping to get a gold medal. It was constantly up hill. It's a lot easier to gather momentum on the way *down* to success, if you know what I mean.

As a child, you hear the story of the little train: "I think I can, I think I can…" It's only when it got to the top it said "I knew I could…" We sometimes need proof to be able to believe. It's a bit like the chicken and egg. Do you believe first then achieve, or achieve then believe?

In Atlanta, our coach was still trying as hard as he could to help us focus on succeeding. I had trouble saying I could win, because I hadn't won before. It's very hard to have that belief, when you have no reason. Only after you get the results do you have the proof. Then is it easy to believe. The runs are on the board. But what if you don't have the results? Does that mean you never will? Then, there is no other choice but to believe anyway!

One of the things I had to adjust was my *attitude to losing*: I needed to realise that, if you don't make it, you're not a bad person, or a loser. Someone was better than you on the day. That's all. You've just got to keep believing. I know now that that's where it starts. There are no losers; only learners. Some people win and say "I don't know how I did it". But somewhere inside themselves, there was a belief they could do it: otherwise they wouldn't have put in all the work to be there in the first place.

It's said that you lose gold to get silver, but as they said on that Sydney Olympic Games commercial, those people have obviously never won silver. It's not just about medals, it's about competition, not only with your opponents, but between you and your own mind. The mind is a powerful force, and when you conquer it, you can achieve anything your heart desires. You can achieve excellence in your chosen field, and the beauty of it is that it's an ongoing process.

The semi-final loss in Atlanta also taught me the value of specific preparation. Kerri and I had prepared for Atlanta by focusing on the American team, Holly McPeak and Nancy Reno. They were the number one team. The

Source: Duane Hart/
Sporting Images

> Ingenuity, plus
> courage, plus work,
> equals miracles.
>
> *Bob Richards,*
> *pole vaulter*

Brazilian team of Jacqui Silva and Sandra Pires also loomed large in our thoughts. All our training, all our role-plays, in the lead-up to the games, was focussed on those players. In our minds, we constantly saw one of those four players. So really, when we beat them, we got what we prepared for! Before the semi-final, Steve, our coach, said (rightly) "If you can beat those two teams, you can beat anybody". But by the time we got to the semi-final, we hadn't spent any time mentally on the Brazilian team we lost to. They were the number two Brazilian team, and ranked fourth in the world.

They were quite different to play, mentally and physically. They served very differently. They were big girls, and played a different style of game to any other team. We hadn't spent enough time visualising their game, and steeling ourselves mentally for what they had to serve up. In other words, we didn't have a mental framework, a 'video tape', if you like, stored in our memory banks, for them. When we

> **The will to win is important, but the will to prepare is vital.**
>
> *Joe Paterno*

stepped out onto the sand, we simply felt as though we were playing someone we didn't know. What a lesson! All it would have taken was a few hours of running our minds and bodies through the experience of playing them, and during the game it became obvious to us that we had neglected this simple, but very important, part of our preparation. We lost to them, and so we got what we'd prepared for!

What's more, The Voice kept saying "You're not prepared, so how can you expect to win?" I even wrote in my diary the night before the match, "One thought lingers…we spent so much time and energy on McPeak/Reno and Jackie/Sandra, we kinda overlooked Monica/Adrianna (ironically, the team that *really* has given us trouble in the past)". Even at that point, I was talking myself into losing.

We were primed to beat the team that eventually won the gold medal—Pires and Silva, and I truly believe that we would have achieved that victory, had we played them for gold. But we never got there, and the best team on the day shone through.

In sporting contests, or in any other 'contest' in life, people intuitively sense fear or a lack of confidence in others, and they become more aggressive. In Atlanta, teams served me 95 per cent of the balls. I'd pass the ball, Kerri would set the ball, and I had to hit it. So I had to constantly apply two skills. They knew. It was as though they could hear The Voice every bit as well as I could! The game was always on my shoulders. In addition, I wasn't as experienced or as skilful as Kerri, and I was eight kilos heavier than I am now.

The heavier that burden became, the easier it was, emotionally, to step out of the way and hear The Voice as it said "You're not good enough Nat!" And the less comfortable I felt, the more comfortable the other team looked. They just seemed to be getting bigger and stronger by the minute, and I started feeling smaller and weaker! Now, I had a lot of thinking to do.

I always had the dream, but I didn't fully realise what it was to dream. To have a vision is one thing; to transform yourself into the sort of vehicle that will *arrive* at that destination is another thing altogether. To master the mind is like putting a plane on autopilot. The plane's still doing all the work, but the guiding intelligence—the pilot—can get on with refining the process even more.

He who stops being better stops being good.

Cromwell

Steve says there are no guarantees

Natalie and Kerri are both what our psychologist classifies as 'thinker/enforcers'. Basically what that means is that they like to lead the ship; they're very certain and confident in what they do. They do it very well. They're very organised. But that kind of certainty needs some sort of guarantee of return. In sport there are no guarantees. The best you get is that you do the hard work, you do whatever possible in your preparation, and you go out onto the court and do your best. That way you have a sort of guarantee: that you will give the best you have. You are not guaranteed a win. Understanding this has been really challenging for them both.

Remember this

- Having a dream isn't enough. It's only the start. What's important is transforming yourself into the sort of vehicle that will allow you to arrive at that dream.

- A dream needs to become a clear vision. Then we can ask ourselves the right question: Is what I am doing now moving me toward the vision, or away from it?

- Anyone can prepare their body. Champions prepare their mind and their spirit as well.

- Learners never lose.

- To achieve our goals, our mind needs to be constantly run through the experience of already being there.

- We need to keep believing, even when we have no proof!

- What matters most is how we see ourselves!

Chapter 6

Seek and ye shall find

Realisation has come to me slowly, via a series of sparks, each one brighter than the one that preceded it. Everyone has an 'aha!' moment, when they come to an understanding that had previously been buried somewhere in their unconscious mind. If you're ready, and receptive to it, it will come. The question then is whether you do anything about it; whether you allow it to take you anywhere. We are confronted with 'once in a lifetime opportunities' at least twice a week. But are we always in the right 'state' to recognise them?

After my Atlanta experience, I wasn't entirely happy, but I wasn't totally deflated either. I was more unhappy before the bronze-medal match than I was after it, and I was determined to revel in the success once we had achieved our Olympic medal. But I was immediately seeking more. I wanted to learn from the experience, so that next time I'd have more tools in my toolbox; more weapons in my armory.

I clearly remember the night the penny dropped for me. The night before our bronze medal match—that is, the night of our loss—everything in my body ached. I was so depressed: I knew we had come so close, yet something was missing—some important piece of information that prevented us achieving our dream.

Something was keeping my performance out of my control. That something turned out to be me. I truly believed it was my destiny to win gold. What I didn't know at the time was that Destiny agreed. It had already said 'yes'. But it had added 'not yet'. I was destined to wait another four years for another opportunity. All we can be sure of in life is that we'll receive opportunities. Once we're in the same position again (if it ever presents itself again), it's up to us to take the plane off autopilot and take the controls.

After our loss, Steve seemed to have tuned out, and only Kerri seemed her normal, chirpy self. We tried to have a team meeting, but I wasn't really interested. Kerri said to me "You're no good to us like this. Go down and get some physio". At 9 p.m. I raced down to the physiotherapist to get some work done on my painful right knee. When I arrived, no one was there. Kieren

Perkins was swimming his famous 1500 metre final, and everyone was gathered around to watch it on the television. All I needed was some attention, and I couldn't get it! So I thought I might as well watch the race as well. Surely you all know the story by now: he'd just scraped in to the final, qualifying eighth, by 0.08 seconds! The whole world had written him off. Except Kieren himself—the only person that mattered.

I clearly remember the sight of him getting out of the pool, veins protruding like the veins of a racehorse. He said to the interviewer that he didn't feel comfortable at all in the water, but was determined to push through it and win, even if his arm fell off. And there I was, thinking "No one believed he could do it. But it didn't matter. All he

> **To succeed, you need something to hold on to, something to motivate you, something to inspire you.**
> *Tony Dorsett*

needed to do was believe in himself". If he'd listened to the press, and everyone else who was amplifying that little voice he probably had in his own head, he would have lost. From that moment I realised "I'm the only one who decides! It's up to me to paint the picture". Funnily enough, I'd already done it before, all those years ago when I decided that girl would never beat me again in the pool. At that moment I made the decision that I would win a bronze medal the next day, and walked back up the stairs.

I'd got just the attention I needed! I didn't need physio.

Somewhere in my mind, a seed that might have been planted a long time ago finally found fertile soil. Looking back on that event, I know now that I was *seeking* inspiration when I went down to watch Perkins swim to that unlikely gold medal. In that respect, it wasn't a chance event. My mind was *prepared* to be inspired, but only on a subconscious level. And there's the difference. If there's anything to learn from that little incident in retrospect, it's this: knowing what I know now, I wouldn't have left it to chance. I would not have *hoped* for inspiration—I would have deliberately sought it much earlier! Today, this is one of the most valuable pieces of advice I could possibly give: *deliberately seek to be inspired*, and it will happen! The rest will take care of itself. Have the radar out, and look to be stimulated, stirred and moved by the successes you see around you all the time. Then find out how they do it.

That event was the beginning of a search that, I know, will never end. I believe the point of it all is the quality of the journey, not the destination—otherwise, a gold medal would have been the end to all my aspirations. It sounds contradictory, but it's not. I can still focus on outcomes. It's the outcome that determines the steps I take—that is, the journey. I've always had inspiring and encouraging friends and family, but today I deliberately try to surround myself with *nothing but* positive people who are *all* inspirational in their own way. Iron sharpens iron, the old adage says, and this has a dramatic effect on your *thinking* and, eventually, on the way you act.

After I went back upstairs, we had our team meeting. This time, I'd decided that tomorrow, we were going to get that bronze medal. I hadn't come here to Atlanta just to swap pins!

> The more I talk to athletes, the more convinced I become that the method of training is relatively unimportant. There are many ways to the top, and the training method you choose is just the one that suits you best. No, the important thing is the attitude of the athlete, the desire to get to the top.
>
> *Herb Elliott*

Chapter 7

Bronze

The fight is won or lost far away from witnesses–behind the lines, in the gym, and out there on the road, long before I dance under those lights

Muhammad Ali

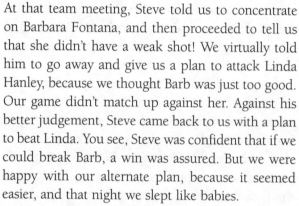

At that team meeting, Steve told us to concentrate on Barbara Fontana, and then proceeded to tell us that she didn't have a weak shot! We virtually told him to go away and give us a plan to attack Linda Hanley, because we thought Barb was just too good. Our game didn't match up against her. Against his better judgement, Steve came back to us with a plan to beat Linda. You see, Steve was confident that if we could break Barb, a win was assured. But we were happy with our alternate plan, because it seemed easier, and that night we slept like babies.

The next day, we followed our plan to a 'T', targeting Linda, who had an answer for everything we threw at her and came back twice as hard. An Olympic medal was the only thing missing from her CV. She is a legend of the sport who had been working on the sands of California for 20 years, and this day she was 'in the zone'. Our master plan wasn't working! I know now that this is because it was born of avoidance and fear. We doubted our ability to break Barb and we took what we thought would be the easy route. If you think you can't, you'll be right!

We reverted to plan A—the plan we didn't think we could execute—knowing full well that when it was over, we would have to eat our words. Steve was right again! He was probably up there the whole time pulling his hair out! Once we settled on Barb, we slowly started to get on top of her. She was, as we told Steve, coming up with all the shots. Because we started on Linda, we were down 9–6. This is when we made the switch. We climbed back from 11–9 down to 11–11 with some tough serves and transition plays. The next point would win the set. It was a scrambled play, and Kerri managed to end it with a well-disguised, unconventional short set over the net. From the moment we changed our plan, we played the game of our lives.

The Voice that had told me in the previous match that we were already beaten had been (at least for this match) subdued. We went on to win the second set 12–7, and at one stage held a 7–1 lead—we were pretty excited about being so close to the win. They came back to 7–6 to loud chants from the partisan crowd: "USA, USA"! My family was in the stands, and in that little gap between the "USA"s, I could hear my dad shouting out "Aussie, Aussie, Aussie".

We pressed on to finish the match strongly. Barb had been very successful the whole match with her arc shot (over my head, to the deep corner) but when it counted, I was ready. I could hear the commentator clearly—it intensified my anxiety and nerves: "Cook with the ball. Bronze medal point, number three". I served to Barb, she went to her faithful arc, I held my ground and dug it, and put it away for the match.

After two hours and six minutes, after experiencing two hard-fought sets, lightning, rain, cold and intense heat, we were Olympic medallists. Seeing the look on Hanley's face, I was relieved again, so glad that it was not me! I could imagine how she was feeling, and wished that there could be one medal each. The reaction after our win was amazing as we faced a whirlwind of press conferences and autographs. Luc Longley was courtside and waiting to congratulate us. What a day! How do you top that? Every day of our lives had been geared toward this event. Now what? In the days that followed I almost felt empty. I almost felt as though I no longer had a purpose. In my diary, I wrote a quote from Louis L'Amour: "There will come a time when you believe everything is finished. That will be the

Although Steve Anderson was, at first, disappointed in our tactics in the bronze medal match, it was also a learning experience for him.

You have to respect their intuition and opinions. My job used to be to coach people. Now, it's to help them achieve their goals. This was the perfect lesson. I'm sitting up in the stands and watching this happen, and part of me says "OK, here we go! Have we really learned this lesson or not?" We had targeted Linda Hanley the whole season and beaten her. But at Atlanta, you could see in her eyes she wasn't going to lose the game. Barbara, however, was showing a few nerves. So when they started on Linda, part of me was a little disappointed that they didn't trust my judgement. But more than that it was like "Ok, well, if we're going to win this match, they're going to have to get back on Barbara and I'm just going to have to trust that through a little trial and error, they are going to figure that out and go with the original call".

beginning". I didn't know at that time just how that was about to apply to my life, but I felt its meaning.

I realised after that day what had been missing. How was it that I was able to suppress The Voice during that match, and not previously? It was then I recognised that it had been my constant companion all those years, giving me poisonous advice on how to sabotage myself and stay in my comfort zone. After that day, I came to the conclusion *that it's only emotional and mental strength that separates the best from the rest*. The strength to fight and never give up is what counts. If only I'd felt that way the day before! In that game, as much as I never gave up physically, my mind was telling me that it was all over. I didn't believe I had the strength to weather the storm. Now a much more hopeful challenge faced me: How do I build on that inner strength?

After the bronze medal win, I wrote to all those people who had been positive, affirming voices in my life: "We couldn't have done it without you and look forward to continuing our relationship through to 2000. As one door closes, another opens. It's the beginning of a bright future for us and the sport of beach volleyball". I knew now what I needed to do.

> **How I use my body, my voice, my eyes, my hands, in addition to the words I use and the way I use words, is my only tool.**
>
> *Bandler and Grinder*

I suppose that if I had to summarise the Atlanta experience and the learning we had gained, I'd have to say that we struggled mentally and emotionally, but didn't make other teams fight for their points. We had only been playing together for 18 months, and our coach, Steve, was trying to create a game that would be effective against any opponents. He had tried to speed up the sets, speed up the offence, keep people off guard. We were not as skilful as other teams, and we had to try to beat them with our power and speed.

Atlanta 1996

This is the moment we have worked so hard for.

I've often been asked the difference between the bronze medal in Atlanta and the gold in Sydney. In Sydney, we had so much power over that little voice. When it spoke up, it was just overridden by an intense desire to overcome all obstacles. By the time we got to Sydney, training felt 'wrong,' because it seemed so easy. It seemed a matter of rehearsing everything physically, then attaching the right emotions to the right situations. Sounds easy, doesn't it? Obviously, getting to that stage took quite a bit of effort, self-realisation, a little pain and a lot of enlightenment.

Steve says

Winning the match is always the ultimate goal, and there are hundreds of ways to achieve it. My aim is to make myself a tool or a resource for people to achieve their goals. The important thing is not to be proved right, but to achieve the goal using whatever is the best path for that particular team or person. Whether it's to work with someone else or to go against my advice, the ultimate goal is what matters. My work is not to teach people what I know, but to help build them into what they need to be to achieve their goal.

Some words on Atlanta, from Steve

My life will never be the same again. Together we have laughed, together we have cried. We have felt the ultimate joy and the ultimate pain. Today marks the end of our journey. We have achieved what few believed we could achieve, what many believed to be impossible and all believed to be remarkable. Only we know the true price for the prize—the blood, the sweat, the tears, facing your fears, the change, the compromises, the desire. You have done all that was asked of you, all that was necessary. And for this I salute you. You have earned the prize. I look back at what we were and where we are now, and I know that every point, every moment of success was paid for. You earned the right to stand tall and be recognised. I am so proud of you. Thank you for your love, your trust, your friendship and for sharing your lives with me. I love you both very much.

Beach volleyball's first-ever
Olympic bronze medals

Remember this

- Taking the path of least resistance all the time means we'll never grow as a result of challenges.

- The worst thing we can do is make plans that are born from the desire to avoid challenges.

- Looking for inspiration beats hoping for it!

- Physical limitations only mean what we allow them to mean; the mind can do anything if we learn to control it.

The Voice: a brief history

I was once asked to treat The Voice as though it was a person; to talk about its history. How it figured in my life and how it influenced me. In short, the hold it had over me, and how I wrestled control from it. Knowing what I now know about the way we listen to our internal voices, I see this as a very important question.

The realisation came slowly to me that The Voice is there for balance. It's there to ensure you don't go too far. It's there, for instance, to ensure you don't jump out of a plane without a parachute (Michael Jordan is the only person I know who can fly)! But if you let it, it will clip your wings so much that you never get off the ground at all. It keeps you with one foot in reality. And if you let it, it will have a greater part of that reality than it deserves.

However, reality is, in a bigger sense, what you make it. Your perception, when you give it truth, is your reality— working for you, The Voice might make you a little more careful about some things. It might say "Don't go and put all your eggs in the one basket. Diversify your investments!" Or "Don't drive on the wrong side of the road, or you'll soon see that there is a reality outside your mind!"

You will never lose The Voice. What's more important is how you react to it, how you treat it, and how often you listen to it.

Back in 1996, The Voice was bigger than Natalie Cook. It was powerful. It had far too much power. It was saying "You're not good enough" and "Who do you think you are?" and "You're too fat, you're too slow". And Natalie Cook would listen to it. After all, The Voice only follows a script written over a lifetime—in this case, my lifetime. It's a composite voice. It consists of the voices of parents, grandparents, friends, teachers, experiences, and accumulated beliefs. It's not that they've all been negative. Some people's Voices have been nothing but positive. But if you've chosen to include in your script all the negative things that have happened to you along the way, then The Voice will read them out to you again and again, as loud and clear as you allow it to! Over time, you will attach truth to it and presto! It becomes your reality.

I'm not sure how my Voice became so powerful and, at times, so negative. What it did back then was keep me in an artificial state of humility. I equated humility with being realistic about my abilities. I guess it's part of our culture, too. We've always tended to confuse confidence and certainty with arrogance. As long as I was listening to The Voice as it was back then, I was never going to win a gold medal. So when the media would ask me if I was going to win, The Voice would tell me to say "We're going to give it our best shot", instead of, simply, "Yes, we have what it takes".

Over the past four years, I've worked at reducing The Voice's share in Natalie Cook, from 90 per cent, to about 10 per cent, if you can put a figure on it at all. I've achieved that by removing the doubts; by looking for ways to prove The Voice wrong; by doing practical things that took courage, because The Voice made me afraid. Things such as firewalking and skydiving. By doing those things, I started to answer The Voice back, saying to it "You are my imagination; you are merely my subconscious, and it's about time you got back in your box. I'm ready to take control now!"

It began to get quieter and quieter. Eventually, it would change its tune. Better to have some influence than none, I suppose. It began to say "Hmmm. That's pretty impressive. Maybe you can do this, after all". It began to become my ally. In other words, I worked not at suppressing it, but at making it say different things. Eventually, it would be saying "Keep going girl, keep going." Occasionally, it might add "But don't go that far". Because I'd made it respect me, I'd start listening to it. It was talking more sense now. Instead of telling me how to do

things, it would begin asking questions. Eventually, it would even start asking the right questions. Questions like "Hey Nat! Is that going to take you towards your goal or away from it?", instead of "Don't eat that piece of cake you fat slob!" When The Voice started to see that I was helping myself, it began to help me. And it was The Voice that would open the door for me, with pleasure, and say "You've found it! Go for it!" So there is still a voice. You can never eliminate it. What I've tried to do is to have it work with me, rather than against me. If you can't control it, it's like a second personality.

Herb Elliott actually sees The Voice as a little man on his shoulder that drives him to keep going. Sometimes it yells at him. He told us in Atlanta that it reminds him of how hard the rest of the world is training. But back then, I was trying to shut The Voice up, and it was demanding its rightful place. One way or another, it will find a way to get out. By the time Sydney came around, we were a partnership, working toward the same goal.

Of course, The Voice isn't really separate from Natalie Cook; it's not separate from you, either. It's just a metaphor. Some call it 'self-talk'. Some say "Experience tells me…" But thinking of it as something separate has helped me to do something about it; to manipulate it to my own ends. You can call all those negative feelings you've brought along from your experience, and your perception of that experience, whatever you like. By calling it The Voice, I was able to change its tune.

Chapter 8

Heroes

I want to make one more point about overcoming negative voices. I've talked about consciously imitating and being influenced and inspired by people whose deeds we admire. There are plenty of people I admire, but I thought I'd mention a few whom you will know.

Firstly, though, I feel I should give my reasons. If The Voice is all about our self-image, we need a way to strive for a self-image that's more ideal for us. Believe it or not, we all do it in various ways. We read magazines and try to be more like the people we admire. As teenagers, we try to dress like our favourite rock stars, and so on. But a lot of this is just empty imitation. You can imitate the outward

Walking the fairway with the Shark

Source: News Ltd

Kerri Pottharst–the passion

form of their lives, but that doesn't mean you're looking for the substance. It's more productive and long-term to try to emulate *qualities*.

The people I've chosen actually tell me a lot about who the ideal Natalie Cook should be! I obviously have a personal scale of values, and they come out when I describe the things I admire about these people. So as you read the list on the next page, try the same thing. Pick a few people (say, three to five) whom you really admire and list their qualities. This list will tell you about the ideal *you*. It will help you to paint a picture of yourself in the future. It will give you something to move towards.

PERSON I ADMIRE	WHY? (ATTRIBUTES)
MICHAEL JORDAN	PASSION
	STRENGTH
	CHARISMA
	AGGRESSION
	DESIRE
	INSPIRES THE WORLD
	HE CAN FLY!
GREG NORMAN	DEFIES THE ODDS
	STAYS ON TOP WHEN PEOPLE SAY HE CAN'T
	HAS GREAT BUSINESS SENSE AND DRIVE
SUSIE O'NEILL	ACHIEVES QUIETLY
	ALWAYS WANTS TO BE HER BEST
KIEREN PERKINS	BELIEVES IN HIS OWN ABILITY
	DETERMINATION
	FOCUS
KERRI POTTHARST	ALWAYS GIVES 100%
	PASSION
	ABILITY TO STAY AT THE TOP FOR SO LONG
	DETERMINATION

It would take a little more effort to then rate the qualities you consider most important, and then ask yourself why. But it's worth it. By deciding to move toward all those attributes with every goal and every action, you will actually be writing yourself a new script. In fact, you'll be rewriting yourself! Try it. Your self-image is a powerful thing.

Remember this

- The language we use to describe ourselves and our attitude to ourselves gives us a clue as to where The Voice is 'at'.
- When we hear negative voices from other people, it's helpful to ask: What else can this mean? How else can this be useful?
- The Voice can be changed, with some effort, as long as we're conscious of the effect it might be having on our life and determine to do something about it.
- We can actively change our self-image by identifying the things we admire in others. It's a great starting point for our life's new story.

Choice/perception

Everything we do—even the emotion we feel at any moment—is a matter of choice. The only reason we feel the same way every time a situation arises is because, of the entire repertoire of emotions available to us, we have attached one feeling to that situation, and haven't even considered that it's possible to feel another way. That's why we're astounded when people who have suffered hardship are prepared to forgive, while we sit there listening to their story and feeling anger or pity on their behalf.

The fact is that once we break a habitual way of reacting to things, those things actually begin to change. People begin to respond differently to us. We restore flexibility to our lives, because we have chosen a different reaction. We have given ourselves the power of choice. Once we get into the habit of choosing our reactions, the length of time between an event and our response to it can seem infinite, as we choose at leisure to respond in the way that best suits us.

The best way to choose a different reaction is to choose a different perception. When an event occurs in our lives, we can perceive it in any way we like, and then base our emotion on that way of seeing.

A friend of mine Peter tells a wonderful story of his ideal date. It goes something like this: "We would be picked up in my air-conditioned chauffeur driven limousine and driven to the most beautiful beach, where we would enjoy a delicious seafood feast as the sun sets over the ocean. My girlfriend and I would talk and laugh as we listen to the waves crash onto the shore. It is a perfect evening". This is the way Peter chooses to look at it. Now look at what Peter realises the reality of this date might be: "We would be picked up on the side of the street by a Brisbane City Council Mercdes Benz BUS. For $2.80 we would go to the beach at Redcliffe for fish and chips". It is funny how the mind can chose to see things. Which way do you choose? The choice really is yours. We should wake up every morning determined to take control of the way we see and feel things. Here's an exercise that may help. Every morning before you start the day, write on a clean page how you intend to approach that day. This provides you with a sense of certainty, purpose and control. Write what you like—use one word or many.

EXAMPLE

Date:

Pro-active

POWERFUL

Persistent

Date:

Smile

Believe in the power of your dreams

Go for gold

Try it!

The way you feel, act and think is your choice.

Choose feelings, actions and thoughts that will empower you, one day at a time.

Part 2

Paving the way with gold

Chapter 9

Learners never lose

An average year followed the Atlanta Games, but something had changed forever in my mind. I'd vaguely begun to realise I was on a journey, and hadn't reached a destination, but now I was more determined than ever to make the journey itself a success.

People ask me how I knew that all these internal changes were working for me, when none of it was translating into results on the sand. After all, we weren't winning tournaments, so it's a fair-enough question.

Change comes in steps. There were three important changes I needed to make, before I even thought about volleyball:
1. body shape and weight
2. my perception of the world
3. a more acute, more sensitive awareness of the world.

Regarding my weight, I'll devote a whole chapter to that later. As for my perceptions of the world, I began to react differently to life's little irritations, such as parking tickets. Once, I'd curse and be in a bad mood all day over something like that. Now, I'd begin to see them as a donation to the council. I was beginning to snap out of the bad moods a lot quicker. I'd begun to learn that there's nothing wrong with swinging from a positive to a negative charge, as long as you don't stay there too long. Mood swings are okay. That's the roller coaster ride of life. The trick is to snap in and out of it quickly.

The third change was really important. I was beginning to develop a more acute, more sensitive awareness to everything: how I view my world, and the way others reacted to it. There is a very important lesson from the movie *The Matrix* regarding awareness. Once you take the red pill, and 'see' everything around you, you can't go back. It is a new world, a new perception. You begin to understand things that you never knew existed. There are no more excuses! It's up to you. In my consciousness, I'd created space that hadn't existed before.

Lastly, I began to notice changes to my volleyball game. I began to 'see' myself applying certain skills before I'd actually applied them. I began to become more consistent. I started to feel stronger, and to hit the ball better. After my volleyball

Source: Duane Hart/Sporting Images

game began to change, people around me, who suddenly had tangible results to relate to, began seeing the positive effects of the decisions I'd made and began to change themselves, almost conforming to my new learnings. I was gaining more respect from the volleyball community and those around me.

In other words, I didn't focus on volleyball, first and foremost. I would have only dug a deeper hole for myself if I'd done that. Someone once said that the definition of a mad person is someone who does the same things over and over, yet expects a different

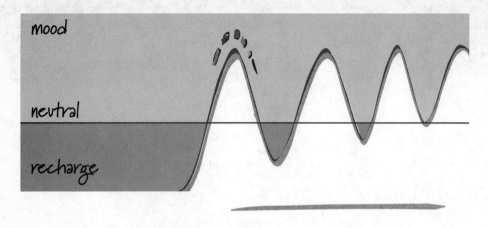

mood

neutral

recharge

Mood swings are ok. The trick is to snap in and out of it quickly

> It's a little like wrestling a gorilla. You don't quit when you're tired—you quit when the gorilla is tired.

Robert Strauss

result! Sounds pretty right to me. To get to a different result you need to make a change. I often say that it's easier to build a new ship than pull the Titanic up from the bottom of the ocean. In other words, start afresh with a clean page.

So, no, we were not winning tournaments, but that can't be considered a failure. For me, personally, failure was beginning to fall away. The idea of failure was beginning to fade, no matter whether we won or lost. I was learning all the time, and the most important learning I was doing was about myself. I couldn't change anything about my volleyball game unless I changed as a person first. Getting through all those games in Atlanta then falling apart when it counted showed me that I had to have a solid foundation. And that foundation was Natalie Cook: the person, not the volleyballer. The thing you can fall back on is the journey; the path to the dream. You can always get back on a path.

To be honest, from this vantage point, it's hard to remember what I once considered failure to be. There is, simply, no such thing. Win or lose, we're the ones who define it, and it probably becomes reinforced at school, where the very words 'pass' and 'fail' become entrenched in our consciousness, and take on all sorts of connotations. Now, those words have almost come to mean the same thing as 'learnt' and 'didn't learn'. Therefore, at school, not reaching a goal means failing, rather than learning. I've worked hard at changing that. Now, not reaching a goal means I need to ask questions such as 'How do I make it better?' and 'What will I do differently next time?' In other words, I want to gain learning from the experience. And as for the fear of failure—the thing I feared was an illusion that I had created.

> **I am an old man and have known many troubles, but most of them never happened.**
>
> *Retrospective wisdom from Mark Twain,*
> *but we don't have to wait so long to gain it!*

> **The mastery of the true self, and the refusal to permit others to dominate us is the ultimate in living, and self-expression in athletics.**
>
> *Percy Cerutty*

Chapter 10

Making the weight

If you've followed our progress, you would have noticed that in Atlanta I was much heavier than I was in Sydney—by eight kilos in fact. I've got skinny arms and legs (so my mother keeps telling me), and I tend to carry any extra weight around my waist. Eight kilos are pretty hard to hide in a bikini! It was a struggle for me. I was training hard. I wasn't eating the wrong foods (or so I thought), and I wasn't eating too much.

The breakthrough for me came when I began seeing a Bicom practitioner. The Bicom is a machine manufactured in Germany. It is widely used in Europe, but rarely in Australia. It can be used to identify and treat allergies without the use of needles or drugs. It's amazingly effective.

I discovered that I was allergic to dairy products, wheat and yeast, and so I cut them out of my diet immediately. Then I began to eat foods that were right for me. I hadn't understood previously how much my own body could tell me about what was happening. Despite all my effort and hard work, I'd forgotten to listen to my body. Every morning I'd wake up and, before long, I'd begin sneezing. I later found out that it was because of the milk I was putting on my cereal. As soon as I cut the milk out, the sneezing stopped. We investigated more and got down to an amazing level of detail. The more I listened to the Bicom practitioner, the more I realised I had to listen to my body in different ways than I had done in the past.

Your body is a garage to park your soul. Treat it with respect.

Source: News Ltd

We identified other food and beverages that were no good for me—things such as pineapple juice and red kidney beans. Even a few of those beans in a salad were enough to set off an allergic reaction. It was a real turning point for me to discover that I could know, in precise detail, what I could safely eat and what I needed to avoid. My energy levels improved dramatically and so did my well being. But most importantly, I began to lose weight. Then, to my despair, my practitioner left Brisbane.

Enter Marcia Pittman. Marcia is able to de-sensitise people to their allergies so that they can, on occasions, actually eat foods to which they were previously allergic or intolerant. In addition to her work with the Bicom, Marcia is also very good at changing people's perceptions, as part of their total well being. She calls it Neuro-emotional Therapy (NET). Neuro-emotional Therapy and its associated discipline of Neuro-emotional anti-sabotage Therapy (NEAT), deals with the emotional components of people's lives that affect their physical, psychological, emotional and spiritual health. The medical profession generally seeks to address emotional issues through either medication or psychiatric counselling, or a combination of both.

When you first see someone like Marcia, or anyone else, for treatment, the ailment you describe to them is called the 'presenting issue'. What Marcia does is go beyond the presenting issue, to the emotional component or components. NET then connects the present experience with the original time in that person's life when the same emotions were experienced. This releases the person from the continued negative impact of both the original and the present factors affecting their well being.

The technique uses aspects of kinesiology (muscle testing) to identify both the emotional components involved and the original time and context in which they were experienced. NEAT expands the NET process by dealing with emotional factors blocking (sabotaging) a person's capacity to function effectively in certain situations. It restores confidence and competence in situations in which people might have been overcome with fear, anxiety or feelings of inadequacy.

Marcia works with people afflicted with everything from chronic fatigue to cancer. And she's kept people alive beyond their doctor's prognosis. The reason she pursued NET is because she found that when someone was adjusted chiropractically, the adjustment often didn't 'hold' due to people's emotional reactions to certain situations. A sore neck, for example, might be caused by the way you react to the kids, not just because your neck is 'out'.

The emotional strength, self-belief and confidence I needed to win in Sydney was heavily influenced by the work I did with Marcia. In the months before the Games, we dealt with a lot of emotional issues, many of which went back to my childhood. She helped me understand why I 'froze' in Atlanta at 3–2. She ended up working with me every day in Sydney, on relationships, family, volleyball, everything.

“
Some people dream of
success. Others wake
up and achieve it.
”

We covered many different issues, but I want to tell you about three that I believe directly influenced the outcome of our quest to win a gold medal. The first issue related to the spectators who flocked to see us play. The stadium at Bondi was a fabulous venue, capable of holding 10,000 people. It was packed for every one of our games. The noise was incredible and the crowd was naturally and overwhelmingly pro-Australian. Kerri and I had never played in front of such a supportive crowd before and when we played our first match, it was quite unnerving. The emotions of the crowd were very audible. They cheered wildly when we won a point, and groaned loudly when we made a mistake. My emotions fluctuated in tune with those in the crowd. At the end of our first match, I was emotionally exhausted.

Marcia was able to help me understand what had happened and prepare me, via NET, to draw on the energy of the crowd as a source of emotional energy for myself, without being sucked into those ups and downs. This made an amazing difference, and I found I could actually connect with the crowd and draw a positive response at crucial moments in the matches that followed. It made a big difference to my attitude and consistency. I'll have more to say about the crowd issue later.

This may sound a bit weird, but the second major issue we dealt with was my tendency to feel sorry for the opposition whenever we were winning and to get caught up in their disappointment to such an extent that my over-sympathetic response was affecting my game badly. Since we were there to win and our goal was gold, feeling sorry for the opposition wasn't all that helpful! Marcia helped me to switch off the sympathy and concentrate instead on winning. Teams playing at Olympic standard are hard enough to beat as it is.

The third area we covered was adjusting my energy levels. Sometimes I'd walk in to see her and say "I've got this cold and I can't shake it". She'd say "It's not a cold. You're reacting emotionally to

Source: Duane Hart/Sporting Images

> We do the strangest things to scuttle our success.
> Whether it's because we're afraid of leaving our nest or
> afraid of failing, we can freeze when it comes time to
> open our wings...be bold.
>
> *Michael Johnson*

something". She made me realise that stress and tension come from within. In a funny kind of way, many of us decide to get sick. *Negative views of the world and negative emotions stress the immune system.* That's a scientific fact.

In my case, we had identified that my physical problems were probably due to a fear of losing. I was asking myself, after a loss, "How do I explain this to everyone else?" *When you ask yourself the wrong question, you'll look for and find the right answer to the wrong question.* And even if you don't consciously know you're doing it, your *body* does.

I got 'scientific' about my body. If I hadn't, I would have been powerless over my prolonged bouts of sneezing, continuing to blame them on 'something in the air'. Often, people who receive good advice say "Well, I'm not giving up milk for anyone.", because it seems such an inconvenient, thing to do. I soon changed that tune when I realised that following Marcia's advice increased my energy level and rapidly improved my general well being.

I wasn't eating the right foods for my body and my blood type, as I'd discovered by reading Cindi O'Meara's book *Changing Habits, Changing Lives*. I had food allergies and didn't know it. I just wasn't listening enough to the messages my body was sending out. When I cut out dairy products, bread, pasta and a lot of the red meats, I lost my excess weight within weeks. Now I'm probably eating *more* 'fatty' foods than I used to, but they're the right foods for my body.

There's one small catch. You still have to work and train hard. My strength and conditioning coach, Phil Moreland, planned a very specific training program that was designed to meet my identified needs. Phil calls himself 'Jack' (of all trades), and looks after our strength, stability, speed and flexibility, as well as the huge task of coordinating other medical support for us. Phil doesn't only make sure we achieve our fitness goals and are more efficient on the sand. He also makes sure we have fun and variety during the hard slog of preparing for tournaments. Phil has taught me that, no matter how monotonous things get as you eat, sleep and breathe volleyball, there is no need to stop enjoying yourself. I couldn't have done it without him. It is very important to have somebody there to keep you on your toes.

Another significant part of my weight loss was Kurek Ashley. Before I met Kurek, who has been my motivation coach and mentor for two years now, I was continually asking myself: "Why am I fat?" He changed that question—it wasn't the right one. Think about it: if you ask yourself "Why am I fat?" you'll only get certain, specific and probably not very flattering, answers, like "because you eat poorly", or "You don't work hard enough". He changed it to "How do I get fit?" or "How do I get healthy?" As you can imagine, the answer varies depending on the question you ask. My question was all about self-image. It was a derogatory question. Furthermore, I thought the solution was to starve my body of foods it might need. By limiting my model of the problem (or my model of the world) I was unable to perceive what it was I needed in order to achieve my goal. The answer to the new questions was all about examining what might be poisoning my body, and what I should do to identify the culprits!

Suddenly my brain, and The Voice inside it, stopped putting me down and started helping me find solutions to new problems. I don't even call it a diet any more. I call it a healthy eating regime, because that's the way I see it. A diet is temporary. A healthy eating regime is a life change. A diet concentrates on eating. My healthy eating regime got to the roots of many other issues I had with myself.

The media has a lot to do with perpetuating myths about diets, because the market for the diet industry is substantial, and each new diet is a new product to sell. Someone always stands to make money from it. In other words the media is a big part of The Voice that drags many of us down. Even those who are not image-conscious can be adversely affected by the media's obsession with image.

Trying harder with the same ideas and the same approach may not solve the problem. You may need to move 'laterally' to try new ideas and a new approach.

Edward De Bono

De Bono also said that a problem is merely the difference between what one has and what one wants. Life presents many problems—I don't mean problems in a negative sense, I mean things to be solved—but *the way we define those problems, the words we use to describe them to ourselves and others, is the only thing that makes the difference.*

When I convinced myself I was 'fat', I tried to 'diet'. When I looked at it as something else, a new solution presented itself. When Kerri and I were looking at the world from the bottom up, it all looked too hard, too much of a climb. As soon as we decided to have a look at it from the top down, things began to change for us and our own actions began to fall in line with this new perception.

> **There are three major sources of energy: food, air and impressions.**
>
> *Brian Tracy*

Goal setting and visualisation also had a lot to do with my sudden, dramatic weight loss. There's a lot to be said for that old 1970s adage 'think thin'. Kurek and I decided on an ideal 'fighting' weight of 72kg. I posted that figure up on my fridge. Whenever I went to the fridge, I say to myself "I'm 72 kilos.", even when I was 78. It was exactly the same as saying in 1998 "I'm a gold medallist." and "I may not be a millionaire now, but I believe I will be, and therefore, I can be". The more you see that vision and the clearer you see it, the easier it is for the brain to go there. You need to make it real, three-dimensional. If it's a new car, you need to smell it, see it, feel it, and hear it. Surround yourself with pictures of the car you want. Test-drive it, even set a date to buy it, then march towards it.

Remember this

- Most of us need to redefine our notion of 'failure'; undo those powerful, negative lessons from school. If we don't reach a goal, it's because we have a learning need. If we still don't reach that goal, it might just be that it's the wrong goal for us, and we need to redefine that!

- If we practice being aware of ourselves all the time, it becomes a habit and a skill. Even when you're just walking along, consciously be aware of yourself and your surroundings.

- The language we use to describe ourselves—to ourselves and others—is what we become. We all need to check it time and time again!

- When we constantly redefine the problem with each new angle, new ideas present themselves.

- We all have to keep that vision in front of us so it becomes clear, in whatever way that works for us as individuals.

Chapter 11

The teacher will appear

Who is this Kurek Ashley character? He's the man who played a big part in changing my life. And he did it by changing the way I see things, the way I see myself.

In a nutshell, Kurek is a peak performance and success coach. He works with people from all walks of life: CEOs, multi-millionaires, elite sports people, drug addicts, rape victims and anyone else interested in reaching their goals or changing direction in their lives.

Kurek is not a 'motivational speaker'. He offers much more than that. The changes he teaches people to make to their lives are cognitive changes, and their effect can be permanent, if they want them to be. He's had a varied life. He used to be a Hollywood actor. While he was doing *Delta Force II*, which  starred Chuck Norris, he was involved in a helicopter crash that killed five men. Kurek carried one of his best friends from the wreckage. His friend was on fire and died in his arms as Kurek tried to administer CPR. For two and a half years, Kurek's life became a living hell of depression. Every night, he put a .357 magnum in his mouth, wanting to

Kurek's first impressions

When I first met Nat I knew I had a true Champion standing in front of me, a hero in the making.

> Genius is one per cent inspiration, ninety-nine per cent perspiration

take the final step and shoot himself. What he couldn't do instantly, he tried to achieve slowly, by drinking and smoking himself to death.

I'm pleased he failed! One day, he woke up. He realised he'd survived that crash for a reason: to inspire as many people on Earth as he possibly could. And so he created a new 'mantra' for his life: How may I serve?

In November 1997, a friend of mine held a success seminar for her company, and asked me if I'd like to come and sit in on it. Kerri and I had ended our partnership by this time, and I took Angela Clarke, my new playing partner, and my coach, Steve. Kurek gave an Anthony Robbins-style, NLP, hypo, American-type seminar. Everything sounded great. It sounded exactly what I needed. You see, I knew that I had what it took to be a champion but I felt something was missing. He had the missing piece to my puzzle!

It might have been a huge coincidence, but then again, everything happens for a reason. Sometime during the seminar, he said "No one remembers who came second or third at the Olympics. Even though that person is third-best in the world, they get no endorsements, no ticker tape parades, no big cash deals. Nothing. The difference between first and third in swimming can be a few hundredths of a second. The difference between first and third is what I call the competitive edge".

He wasn't to know that I had a bronze medal. So at the end of the seminar I said "Excuse me sir. I'm the one who stood on the third-place box. No one remembers who I am, but I'm Natalie Cook. Nice to meet you". Kurek was a little apologetic, and went on to assure me that it was a fantastic achievement. I was—as I tend to be—quite direct with him. I cut him off with "I don't want to hear any of it, but thank you anyway. I'd like to talk to you about going to Sydney and standing in the first position on that dais". But I also admitted he wasn't far from the truth, saying: "It was exactly the way you said it was. It was dead quiet the next day, and it stayed that way

for quite a while. I think you may be the missing link we've been looking for". We then walked across the road and had a coffee, and from that day, he started with the team.

He's always had some different ways about him. At first, he told us that if we didn't give it all we had, he'd be gone. He introduced a 'fine' system into our training plan. If he gave us a tactic or strategy, we had to have done it before our next meeting. If not, we'd be fined $5,000! We agreed, but only because we knew we had no choice! He was serious and we knew it. So we always made out that we had done it, even if we hadn't and, believe it or not, we thus became masters of his first precept: Fake it till you make it! We never had to pay once, and it's just as well, as I would have been broke after the first week. I thought half his tools were a load of rubbish!

Kurek describes his role in my life.

When Nat asked me to help her, it took me all of two seconds to say "Let's do it!". But I also said "You need to know that I am going to push you to your limits and beyond. I am going to get you to do things that are going to seem crazy. You are going to have to do whatever it takes". I worked with Nat, and eventually Kerri, at least twice a week for the next two years. My job was like that of a stone sculptor. I chipped away, little by little, at their layers of disbelief. I knew that the champions were in there all the time.

In the early days there were rough patches. Nat would become frustrated and scream out, "Why isn't this garbage working?" Both of them wanted to win gold badly—there was never any doubting their desire. But they were still loaded with self-doubt and fear that they would fall short of their goals again. I had to get them to understand that courage is not the absence of fear. It is driving forward in spite of it.

As Muhammad Ali said "Don't tell me I can't do something, don't tell me it is impossible. Don't tell me I am not the greatest. I am the double greatest!"

> **If he is indeed wise, the teacher does not bid you enter the house of his wisdom, but rather leads you to the threshold of your own mind.**
>
> *Kahlil Gibran*

Kurek doesn't like to be called a 'motivation' coach, because motivation comes and goes. He's led me to the threshold of my own mind, and that's been priceless. But it was my own desire to learn that gave me the courage to approach him in the first place. I had to seize the moment, or it might have disappeared forever. Because I was on the lookout for inspiration, I felt compelled to approach him. Don't get me wrong. I could have listened to The Voice. I could have said to myself, "This man's too busy to listen to somebody that no one remembers because she only came third". A lot of us tend to do that. Our shyness or reluctance to approach someone is actually a function of something else that's going on inside our heads.

But, I guess that Kurek would have wanted to know, above all else, that I was teachable and that I had the desire to learn, and he wasn't going to know anything if I'd just sat back and kept quiet. What I had to ask him was no small task: it was to be the best in the world at something by a given date: 25 September 2000. I asked him to be a part of it.

People might think I approached him with an attitude. I did—it was an attitude of learning and a burning desire to do better. Every human endeavour begins with an attitude.

Kerri on belief and confidence

In Atlanta I clocked the fastest serve, at 77km per hour. If my memory serves me correctly, I served the most aces as well . . . but I also probably served the most errors. I believed that I could serve really hard but not accurately. No one ever told me any differently. When Kurek came along he encouraged me to believe that I could be accurate and consistent . . . and continue to serve hard. We experimented with all kinds of visualisation and positive reinforcement during training, using small targets, and within a few weeks my serving had improved out of sight! With this came more belief and confidence and with that came more aces.

Source: Duane Hart/Sporting Images

Remember this

- Looking at life from the top down, rather than the bottom up, helps us to be clearer about the steps we need to take. Describe to yourself your ideal situation, then live as though it's already happening. What do you need to do? What do you need to stop doing?

- If we put no limits on our 'model' of the world, no perception will be closed to us.

- Everything begins with an attitude. If it prevents you from learning or making progress, it may need to be reassessed and changed. Before you're faced with a task, ask yourself about your attitude to it.

- Sometimes, your ego or your fears stop you from submitting to others who have done more learning than you. It's better to gain from the learning of others who have been there than to 'reinvent the wheel'.

- Act as if you've already achieved your goal, and others will treat you that way. Fake it till you make it!

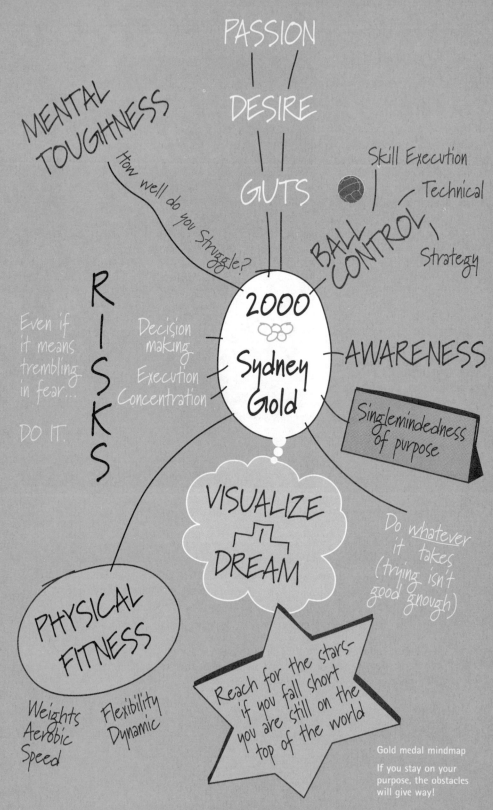

PASSION

DESIRE

GUTS

MENTAL TOUGHNESS

How well do you struggle?

Skill Execution
Technical
BALL CONTROL
Strategy

2000 Sydney Gold

Even if it means trembling in fear...

DO IT.

R I S K S

Decision making
Execution
Concentration

AWARENESS

Singlemindedness of purpose

VISUALIZE
DREAM

Do whatever it takes (trying isn't good enough)

PHYSICAL FITNESS

Weights
Aerobic
Speed

Flexibility
Dynamic

Reach for the stars— if you fall short you are still on the top of the world

Gold medal mindmap

If you stay on your purpose, the obstacles will give way!

Chapter 12

The structure of dreaming

Whenever I have a dream, I like to draw it on a piece of paper. I create a picture. This is a powerful tool that works for me. I'd like to say I sit there for half an hour every day and visualise, but I don't. It would suit a lot of people to do that, and if it works for you, go for it! But I need to see something concrete and not merely confine it to the mind's eye.

I've found over the years that my mind is too restless. Sometimes, if I do 'visualise' in the strict sense, I hit the fast-forward button and speed it up, getting it over with in a minute. That still works. Sometimes, I'll play with it in slow motion. But generally, I get bored, because I like to begin with the big picture. I like to go straight to the end product; straight to what I want or desire. That doesn't mean the process isn't important. But if you don't know where you're headed, it doesn't matter which path you take. I want to see the outcome in front of me all the time. It inspires me to keep moving forward. That's why, after Atlanta, I bought an Olympic gold ring that I wear whenever I play. Every time I dive into the sand and don't want to get up because I'm too tired or it's too hard, I look down at my finger and it fires me up to work even harder.

I also make my dreams 'holistic'. I don't just want to dream about success on the sand. I try to see my life as a wheel or a pie chart, and break it up into different areas, or pieces of the pie, that I'd like to work on: things such as fitness, relationships, finances, lifestyle. I try to make all those areas equal, because if one area's out, the wheel tips over. I might be spending more *time* doing volleyball, but I don't place it above the others in importance. This was a problem after Atlanta. Volleyball *was* my life, and there was no balance.

I also try to create 'ultimate scenarios'. For example, I'll ask myself: "If I had the money to do all the things in life I want to do, what would I do?" I place no restrictions on the answers. I want to be as free as I can to release those dreams. When I've written down everything I want to do, I prioritise my top five. They're the things I go after so strongly that the rest tend to fall into place anyway.

When I really thought about it, I didn't *specifically* want a gold medal. I wanted to feel like a gold medallist—what it would bring into my life and the

" An idea, to be suggestive,
must come to the individual
with the force of a revelation "

lives of others, and what I could accomplish as a result. There was a much greater purpose behind it. I pictured that purpose in the following way.

I was not only striving for a gold medal and all it represented, I was also striving for *Gold Medal Excellence (GME)*. GME is maintaining a golden standard in all areas of your life. Everything from family, to friends, to business and of course volleyball. By striving for GME, the journey itself becomes golden, and then the rest of my life also feels good. We developed this concept at camp—our final team gathering before heading onto the world tour. We were building an energy field around us so powerful that it swept everyone around us into its orbit.

People often ask "What would have happened if you hadn't won?" I always say that regardless of the outcome, it was a golden journey and that cannot be taken away from me. By creating such an energy field around us, we gave ourselves a greater chance to succeed.

Sit down and draw. Paint. Colour in. Or, if it suits you, write. But just make sure you get all the details so you can see them, feel them, smell and taste them.

I believe that if you start at the top and work backwards, the universe will somehow find a way for you to stay there. If your perceptions are a major source of energy, then this is a universal law that applies to everyone, yet it seems to be one of the best kept secrets. It's time we began to take this vital truth more seriously than we have to date.

> This entire planet is made up of energy. The atoms of air surrounding it are energy. The sun pours energy upon this air and upon this earth. Life depends on energy; in fact, life is energy.

Henry Grady Weaver

Source: News Ltd

Having a dream isn't just an airy-fairy concept. 'Having' a dream means doing things to attain that dream. Maybe that's another way of looking at Kipling's words: "If you can dream, and not make dreams your master". In other words, dreaming all day is just that: daydreaming. There's something in that Nike slogan, 'Just Do It.' Nothing else matters as much.

We will always try to justify in our own minds, with the help of The Voice, why things will not work in our lives. I often tried to put that one over Kurek: "I've tried that, and it didn't work". And he'd reply, "Well, yeah, but you only tried it for one hour! Let's try it for *ten* hours and see if it works". In fact, a lot of literature today tells us that we need to practice something for 21 days before it becomes a habit. That includes anything: giving up smoking;

Success is the sum of small efforts repeated day in and day out.

Robert Collier

Source: News Ltd

Our greatest weakness lies in giving up. The most certain way to succeed is to *always* try something one more time.

Thomas Edison

changing our reactions to a given situation; going for a run in the morning. Absolutely anything. Here's a challenge for you. Say, "For twenty-one days, I will…[you fill in the rest!]"

I was at the stage where I not only had to try things—I had to really believe in what I was doing. Believing is often considered some sort of namby-pamby idea, without a structure or a strategy. But believing, like dreaming, is a matter of practice. When I look back at movies that have been an influence in my life, such as *Star Wars*, for instance, I realise that there were messages in them that I picked up along the way because I sought inspiration. At the Sydney Olympics I had a poster of Yoda on the wall. On the poster was written all the wisdom of Yoda, every single thing he says in the entire *Star Wars* trilogy. One thing sticks in my mind:

 There is no try, only do.

Yoda

At practice, Steve used to tell me to do things and I'd protest, "I'm *trying*". And he'd say, "I know you're trying. Now just stop trying and start doing it!" It really is that simple. Just do it! The young Jedi Knight, Luke Skywalker, said to Yoda, "I don't believe I can do that." Yoda shook his head and replied, "That is why you fail".

Sometimes, the thing that stops us doing is our past. The past can be paralysing. But when you start saying to yourself that *there is no history*, and that *I'm me and I'm now*, then your brain is no longer trying to justify failure and consequently you don't expect it. You start driving that vehicle by looking through the windscreen, instead of the rear-vision mirror. What we tend to do is build ourselves up from *what we were*, as though that is also *what we will always be*.

A friend of ours wrote down a quote on a scrap of paper and gave it to Kerri to take to Sydney. "Be ready at any moment to give up who you are in order to become who you could be." I thought,

"Yes! That's exactly why we're here". During the entire two weeks of the Sydney Games, I constantly reminded myself that I am who I am; that I have fears and doubts, and if I give all that up, what could I become? Nelson Mandela says it's our light, not our darkness, that most frightens us, because we don't know how powerful we can be. *Once you decide there is no history, you can move forward at a cracking pace*. Realising that was a powerful experience for me. Getting into the subconscious and changing the programming of the brain is not an easy thing to do. It takes work; it takes *doing*. It takes replacing one habit with another, destroying old videotapes and making new ones.

All this was beginning to happen to me, but there was no structure to it. I was just bouncing through. When I met Kurek, he provided that structure by

> **Treat a man as he is and he will remain as he is.**
> **Treat a man as he should be and he will become**
> **as he can and should be.**
>
> *Goethe*

providing a purpose for it all. What he helped me to do was to find a new assembly point; a new way of looking at my dreams and beliefs. The dream was born—it was to win an Olympic gold medal—but I had been chasing it from the wrong direction: from below. I used to write myself lots of inspirational quotes and self-affirmations, but they didn't work. When I came to Kurek I said "Look, I *tried* to say I was going to win. I *tried* to say I was the best". But somewhere, down in the core of my being, I didn't believe it. I wasn't buying into the talk.

That's because I'd learned, but I hadn't learned enough to be the Natalie Cook I wanted to become. While process of transformation had begun, a lot of the old Nat was still there, making self-fulfilling prophecies about herself. As long as she was saying "I can't win.", she wouldn't; as long as she was saying "this is impossible", it was.

Whether you think you can or think you can't, you're right.

Those words reveal a lot about how we can motivate ourselves. History is full of examples of how people have been fed positive messages about themselves from others, and have succeeded beyond their own expectations. If it's possible for people to inspire us from the outside, then it's even more possible for that inspiration to come from within. Why wait until someone comes along? They may *never* show their face! It's great to get the approval of others, but not everyone knows what we're capable of as well as we do ourselves, so they might not even know what to encourage!

The ironic thing in my case is that I needed someone to show me how to motivate *myself*. Kurek didn't come into my life just to keep giving me encouragement. He wasn't trying to make me dependent on him for motivation; he was trying to help me find the inner resource of motivation that I could take with me anywhere, whether Kurek was there or not. You couldn't ask for a more valuable gift!

> **Catch a man a fish and you feed him**
> **for a day; teach him to fish and you**
> **feed him for a lifetime.**

Remember this

- There is no history; keep moving forward.

- Dreaming and believing are not just things that happen inside your head; doing them is what makes them real.

- Set your goals and visualise them in the way that suits you best.

- We should always try to be 'holistic' about our dreams; to include all aspects of our life.

- Dreams do not become real to us until we can see them. Writing them down is vital. We have to do something for 21 days before it becomes a habit.

- Depending on others for approval can make us fall short. While it's great to get approval, for some of us it may never come!

- The aim of learning is to catch fish for yourself. Learning is doing!

- Asking ourselves: "What motivates me?" gives us something upon which to act.

Chapter 13

The beginnings of change

Kurek wasn't the only one getting us to do outrageous things in practice.

Like Kurek, our coach Steve also believes that low self-confidence is one of the biggest barriers to winning. "I had the girls barking and crowing like roosters in the middle of Southbank, Brisbane, with people watching", he laughs. "I had the experience myself, as a player, of getting out there and somehow being ashamed to give my all, in case I failed; as though it's better to make half an effort, and say 'I'm not really fully committed to this'. There's something almost embarrassing about going all out. But champions don't care. They respect themselves; they respect their work. And every time they get on the court, it's everything to them—they're passionate

Change is a funny thing. There's a whole industry built around implementing change, motivating people for change, getting people excited about it. But a lot of efforts at change fail. People go along to seminars, and get incredible emotional 'highs' for a weekend. They come to realisations about themselves, and they hear things about themselves they've never heard before. But the problem with a lot of the change books, seminars, conferences and training sessions, is that the effect often doesn't last. Change barely occurs. People return to their routines and everything is the same as when they left. While they have all this new knowledge, they get discouraged because the rest of the world doesn't seem to conform to their new vision of that world.

And so, the memory and the exhilaration fades and life settles down again and becomes as it was before. That's why I was always cynical about 'motivational' techniques. 'Quick fixes' don't work. I was searching for *permanent* change: the type of change that would not only win me a gold medal, but would allow me to seek and achieve excellence in every endeavour in life.

 Don't put people in boxes. Give them responsibility. Not goddamn rules!

Michael Conway

about what they do, and they don't care who's watching and what they think. Champions express themselves through their sport and through doing what they do best, playing it. With the Southbank episode, my message to Nat was 'Commit to what you do. No matter how embarrassing'. Getting past the embarrassment and committing to the task is the same as playing volleyball. You're exposed anyway. You're naked out on the court in front of a crowd. People see so much of your character. So why be out there and only make half an effort, holding something back? You better believe that the people beating you are not holding anything in reserve. They're putting it all on the line."

I saw Kurek four times a week. At first, I thought a lot of his stuff was hype. My mind was a little closed. I had my own beliefs, and I told myself that his methods simply were not going to work for me.

Initially, we went through a lot of stuff about identity, celebrating mistakes, celebrating learning. He actually wanted me to physically celebrate when I did something wrong! And I said "No. I can't do that". I understand now that it takes something as radical as that to break old mindsets, entrenched ways of thinking, and habits that cling like barnacles. You have to prise them off!

Ego can be the greatest barrier to learning. After all, how can you celebrate mistakes when you don't even like admitting you're wrong, or when you see mistakes as failures? So, there was Kurek, standing on the side of the court trying to make me celebrate every time I made a stupid mistake, and I'd be yelling back at him. We'd be yelling at each other! Kurek just wanted us to play full out. His theory is that the harder you resist, the harder you fall. I was beginning to see that myself. I certainly wasn't improving by using my own methods. It was that mad-person behaviour again: doing the same thing over and over, yet expecting a different outcome!

I had chosen Kurek as a teacher. I was the one who approached him, so eventually I decided to do everything he asked, at first feeling like a clown. But after a short time I *really* started doing what he asked. Soon I started to see changes in the way I was playing. It was another one of those "aha!" moments. Sometimes change comes in small steps. Sometimes it comes in an instant.

Remember this

- Celebrating mistakes—even quietly—helps us to see that a mistake is only an opportunity for new learning.
- We must open our minds if we're to succeed; always try to have a childlike curiosity.
- 'Quick fixes' don't work. Change requires new habits, and habits, bad or good, develop over time. Build and nurture the good ones.

Chapter 14

Paving the way

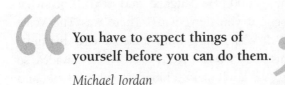
You have to expect things of yourself before you can do them.
Michael Jordan

I want to start this chapter with a parable that is particularly meaningful to me. A group of travellers in the desert came across Moses and thought their luck had changed. They raced over to him and begged for rain. Their village was dying because of the drought. Moses said "Go my friends and there will be water". So they left, excited, thinking that the rain would come. It didn't, so they went back to him and said "Moses, you sent us away with the reassurance that there would be rain. But it has not come". Moses said "You want rain?" "Yes", the people answered. "Well where are your ditches?" Moses replied. "Ditches?" The villagers were puzzled. "Yes, your ditches. How can I give you rain if you have not dug your ditches in order to catch the rain?"

If you want something in life, you have to prepare yourself to receive it. If you want a car, you have to arrange a space in your garage, or even build a garage. If you want money, you open a bank account.

The first thing Kurek got Angela and me to do was to buy a cabinet for our gold medal. At first, I laughed at him. But, because of the way I was beginning to program myself, through Kurek's constant teaching, it must have registered with me.

Kurek points out the importance of aiming high.

Kerri once asked me, "Hey Mr Positive Goal Setter, our goal last time was to win gold—and we fell short and got bronze. What can you possibly do differently this time?" I told them, "We are not aiming for gold. If you aimed for gold last time and got bronze, then this time we are aiming for diamond-platinum". When you see your goal as the end of the journey, you set yourself up to fall short, to not get what you want. The key to getting what you want is to aim way past your goal, so that if you fall short you wind up with the goal that you wanted all along. Shoot for the stars; if you fall short you are still on top of the world.

One day, about two weeks later, I walked past a pet shop. I was thinking, 'cabinet = upside-down fish tank', whereas Angela's perception was 'big glass cabinet'. I decided the fish tank was going on top of my television set. The pet shop didn't have the tank I wanted. So I went to the guy who made the fish tanks, and gave him my specifications: hexagon shape, about 20 centimetres high, wooden base, gold trimming. He looked at me as if I was an alien and said "What the bloody hell do you want that for?" I explained that it was for my gold medal from Sydney 2000. He laughed and said "And what happens if you don't win?" There was The Voice again! It was coming from someone else this time. By this stage, I wasn't ready to entertain that idea, so I said "Well, it'll make a bloody good fish tank, and if it leaks, I'm bringing it back!"

I cleared the space and put the tank on top of my TV. Then Kurek said "Fill it with gold". So I put in it gold medals from the past, the Erricson Cup soccer gold medal of our strength and conditioning coach Phil Moreland, gold Easter eggs, a gold candle with Sydney 2000 on it—any gold trinket I could find. But it didn't end there. I was beginning to understand what Kurek was getting at. I wasn't going to just confine myself to a fish tank. I wanted to fill my life with gold. I wanted to attract gold! I bought a gold camera, gold toothpaste, gold toothbrush, even gold boxer shorts! Around my neck, I wore a gold coin, because I wanted to feel that gold around my neck. That coin symbolised the gold medal for me. I really bought into the belief that if I surrounded myself with gold and that was all I saw, then I would go gold. I even cut a real-sized gold medal from gold paper, and put it on my mirror at just the right height, so that, whenever I brushed my teeth, I would see a gold medal around my neck.

Of course, people laughed. But after a while, they began to play along and buy me golden gifts. But, more importantly, the ploy was beginning to work for me. It began to create such a powerful feeling in my

Without vision, people perish.

mind and my body that I felt I was never going to lose. Now, people ask me "What if something had gone wrong and you didn't win?" It's a valid question. After all, we hadn't won an event up until then. We'd come second, third, fifth…but we had never actually won. Well, we had won one World Tour event, but the Brazilians were missing. It was a win we never even bothered to include on our bios. But I'd seen that vision for so long—that wave crashing in on Bondi Beach, the sights, sounds, smells—that there was no other option. We were going gold. It was etched in my mind like a groove in a record. This is the new identity we created for ourselves. It was a script we read every day.

Today, tomorrow and every day I re-commit myself to being the champion that I have chosen to be.

I am a gold medallist!
I am a champion!

I will have fun always because a positive attitude gives me access to passion, courage, balance, respect and all of the other universal powers that a champion uses.

As a champion I promise to always participate at 100% of my potential from the beginning of the tournament to the end.

I appreciate that each member of the team always contributes 50% to the result of the team and that without the support and the participation of my team member I would not have the opportunities I have now.

I will always work together with my team mates toward accomplishing our goals.

I am the master and creator of my universe and I am responsible for peaking when it is time to peak.

I here and now commit to doing what is necessary to achieve success.

I am a champion. My partner is a champion.

We inspire and empower each other to be the best we can possibly be.

We set our own standard.

When my partner does something great I am happy and I am inspired to greatness because I know that together, at our best, no one in the world can stand in our way.

This is what I believe and this is what I know.

I AM A CHAMPION!
I AM A GOLD MEDALLIST!

Remember this

- Prepare space in your life so you're ready to receive the things you desire.
- Having a dream isn't enough. We need to do as much as we can to put ourselves inside that dream. Immerse yourself in the dream.
- Worrying about what other people think is useless! Their dreams and goals are not yours. Don't concern yourself with what others think. It's what you think that matters. Your voice has the power to override others.

Chapter 15

Fire and glass

I mentioned earlier that I had decided to do everything Kurek asked. But there were times when I definitely thought he was stretching the friendship!

How many tasks have you stood in front of, in reality or in your mind's eye, and thought they were impossible goals, insurmountable obstacles to your progress? Have you looked at the wealthy and wondered why they were born that way and you weren't, or considered your genetic makeup and decided that you're just not gifted? Have you run your mind through fearsome experiences, such as facing a fast bowler, fighting Mike Tyson, or making a public speech?

So have I. Many times. As far as beach volleyball goes, though, for me it was the Brazilians. I've stood in front of them many times and thought I could not possibly beat them.

> **The first and great commandment is, Don't Let Them Scare You.**
>
> *Elmer Davis*

If I thought they were impossible, then it was likely there were many other things in my life I thought I'd never overcome, but which were, in fact, achievable.

One of them was walking barefoot across burning coals, at a temperature of 600 degrees celsius, glowing with heat and glowering at me, daring me to even think about walking across them. The firewalk is not a gimmick. It is symbolic. In people's minds, fire is a symbol for the impossible, the perilous. People talk about difficulties using terms such as 'jumping through hoops of fire'. They talk about danger in terms of 'playing with fire'. The firewalk is

Steve on the firewalk

Everything we did, I did first and this, to me, is what it is all about. You can't ask someone who is trusting you to lead them to do something if you are not doing it first and telling them they are going to be OK.

The fist became a powerful anchor.

important for participants in Kurek's seminars and workshops. By the time it comes around, people will already have asked and answered a lot of fundamental questions about themselves: their values, motives, fears and obstacles.

At the start of the day of a firewalk, many people say "I'm not doing the firewalk. *I'm not doing the firewalk*". They are missing the point. It's not about overcoming a heap of hot coals; it's about overcoming yourself. So Kurek says, "Great! You're not *here* to do the firewalk! But if I'd told you we were doing a seminar on communication skills, and personal development, you wouldn't have come. So I have to call it a firewalk. But you don't *have* to do it, and you will!"

By the end of the day, about 95 per cent of people end up walking across those searing hot coals. They come to understand that by doing so, they will have committed to moving forward in their lives and stepping over the fears, doubts and obstacles that they have thrown into the fire. Before we did the firewalk, Kurek taught us about 'anchoring'—attaching a *feeling* to a physical act—so that, on command, we could create that feeling any time we liked, just by doing the physical act, which is called the 'power move'. Once you do this, you go straight into 'the zone'.

I was scared. I made sure, as we lined up to do the walk, that I was halfway down the queue so I could see how everyone else was doing! I was still wrestling with some doubts when my turn came. Kurek was there waiting. He looked me in the eye and said "What would it mean to you to have a gold medal?" Immediately I felt my physiology change. My shoulders went back, my head went up, my chest lifted. Kurek stepped out of my way and I marched across the coals. In hindsight, it was easy, but that's not the point. I was nervous and apprehensive one moment; the next I felt like Superman. I had not only firewalked, I had taken the first and most important step toward achieving my goals. The journey had begun. Internally, I would never be the same again, and that's the whole point of the exercise.

Source: News Ltd

Look mum, no burns!

I've since guided eight-year-old kids across hot coals, and their lives have never been the same. I keep in touch with some of them, and whenever they think they can't do something, it's only necessary to say to them "Of course you can! You're a firewalker. You can do anything!" And their eyes light up. It's not the sort of thing you learn at school. The firewalk is about leaving our comfort zones. It's also about taking the *first* step. Because after you've taken that, you'll take the rest pretty rapidly. Those coals are damned hot!

> " **Progress always involves risks. You can't steal second base with your foot still on first.** "
>
> *Frederick B. Wilcox*

After Kerri and I split, Steve noticed the beginnings of transformation.

After Kurek came on board, Nat transformed into a different person. He had a tremendous effect on her as a person and on her ability to access her talent when she needs it. Nat was maturing in a tough situation: she was under the intense pressure of representing her country and she was playing with Kerri, a dynamic player ten years her senior and a former captain of the national indoor team—in short, an athlete who commands a certain amount of attention and respect. There was a time when people put Nat down in comparison to Kerri, who is such a dynamic hitter. Under that sort of pressure, it is very easy to crumble. But Nat would rise to the occasion even when she was trembling with nerves.

I'll come back to firewalking in a minute, but first I want to say a little bit more about learning.

There are many different dimensions to learning, and one of the most important is wisdom. They say that intelligence is the narrow view while wisdom is the broad view. How many people have you met who gain new learning, but don't carry it very well? They become know-it-alls, judgemental of people who aren't in the same place. This is despite the fact that the place other people occupy is probably just as good for them. Even if it isn't, people don't listen if you're bombastic with your advice. What you are yells at them so loudly, they can't hear what you say. Fortunately for my sake, I realised this early enough to save the precious partnership with Kerri Pottharst that led to a gold medal in Sydney. But it took serious self-evaluation first.

After our history-making result in Atlanta, Kerri and I sat down and mapped out where we wanted to go from that point. We were excited about the year ahead, and thought we could become the best in the world and take the number-one ranking. Despite all our best intentions, things began to go wrong: our performance was not meeting our expectations. We started finishing fifth, seventh, and even ninth in some cases. We began pointing the finger at each other and not enjoying our journey.

Kerri was 10 years older and trying to fill the roles of sister, friend, business partner and volleyball partner. At the age of 21, I may have resented Kerri's

role and experience, rather than according it the respect it deserved. Kerri and I needed to split up; we needed to go our own ways and I needed to go out and learn things on my own. We realised that if there was any chance of us playing together in Sydney and achieving our dream of turning our bronze into gold, this was our only option. We went our own ways wishing each other luck and agreeing that if we got back together, it was meant to be. But on some level, I think we believed, sadly, that it would never happen. I was a little 'freaked out' when we split. I realised I was on my own more than ever before. One enormous revelation I had when I was with Angela was the way that teaching other people reinforces your own learning. I realised what Kerri had been trying to do with me. Angela was new to the beach, with loads of potential, and I found myself filling all the roles Kerri had tried to fulfil with me. I realised that I had been looking at my relationship with Kerri the wrong way. Acting as a mentor figure to Angela helped me to clarify the lessons I was trying to impart. Imagine reading a book and trying to remember every detail of what you've read. Unless you have a very good memory, it would be very difficult. But imagine that you have to deliver a lecture or lesson about the book's contents. You will be much more likely to organise the information in a way that that helps you to understand it and make sense of it for others. After a while, you become what you teach. My experience with Angela was like that.

A while before Kerri and Nat split, Herb Elliott told us, as a team, "Do it trembling, but do it". Nat's always had that ability, but now she's got the added bonus of being comfortable with uncertainty.

Kerri on our reunion

Splitting up was a turning point for us both. We went on our own journeys, gathered our own experiences. When we reunited we realised how valuable that time apart had been, and we understood that our chemistry, as a partnership on the court, was still there. In fact it was even stronger because of our experiences apart.

Steve says that coaching can be a lonely profession.

There's only one thing I regret saying. It was in Italy. I was challenging Nat and Kerri. They weren't taking responsibility for their performance and they were blaming each other. I think I told them they were gutless. They were really hurt. In that moment I realised that I had overstepped the mark. My one rule is that you don't push people to their breaking point. I've got a responsibility to take care of the people I work with. If they look like they are going to break, I back off and encourage them to have fun. Kerri and Nat both basically said "Screw you. If you don't believe in us, who needs you?" And I was thinking "Oh boy. That's not what I meant". That was hard to deal with, and it took me a while to come to terms with.

Sometimes, as a coach, you've got to be the person who forces athletes into a place that is uncomfortable for them. And who wants to do that? It sucks! I came to terms with it and thought, "I can't be the damn nice guy all the time". It's a part of coaching that I really don't like and that I had to master. Because when you get people out of their comfort zones you get major results.

Anything is possible

It damages relationships. I'd like to be friendly and happy and have fun all the time. But when you cause pain to people you work with, it's really difficult to socialise with them: understandably, they find it hard to separate the things you do at work from the person you are socially. But that's the sacrifice I make because that's the job. Coaching can be one of the loneliest professions in the world. The mission of the team has to take precedence over individual feelings.

During a tournament in Gstaad, Switzerland, we had a real barney in the stands after a match. Kerri and Nat told me they were disappointed and upset about certain things in our relationship, about the way things were going, and about the fact that they weren't getting results. I got up and kicked a chair...I just about broke my boot on it. I was genuinely angry. There wasn't a lot of trust at that point, and we had been through some pretty rocky times. I didn't feel that they respected me or appreciated what I was giving them.

Normally I don't mind someone telling me what they think of me, even when it's not complimentary. I usually say, "OK, let's work on that". But in this instance, unfortunately, my ego became involved. My mission as a coach is to do whatever it takes to help

I consider it a major stepping stone for me and an invaluable lesson.

In July 1999, when Kerri and I got back together, we agreed on one thing: we were destined to go on and win that gold medal. The next step was to find the best way to do it. I immediately wanted Kerri to experience everything I'd been through, as it was such a powerful and effective experience for me. I really wanted her to experience the inner changes that come about as a result of the firewalk. I may have pushed too hard at first. Kerri chose not to do the firewalk, and hesitated at jumping blindly back into the team. In her absence it had become, by default, my team, and naturally she didn't want it that way. In order to be successful, we needed to come back together as equals.

I tried hard to let her know that she didn't have to imitate me and take my path. There was no need. Kerri knows her own mind and she was already a huge success. She probably didn't need any help. She had the fastest serve at the Atlanta Games and had been playing both forms of volleyball for a long time. She felt she didn't need to do the firewalk, and she was probably right. People find their own paths. But initially I was resentful of her decision and perhaps a little judgemental. I had to change those feelings. I was so anxious to share my new learning with her, and we had so little time left, that I decided the best way to do it was to lead by example; to demonstrate the learning I had gained, and not just spout the theory.

A lot of fortunate things happened along the way to Kerri's eventual participation, on her own terms, in some of the teachings that had been so important to me. Kerri uprooted everything for the sake of the team, moving to Brisbane from Sydney. Following a serious knee injury that ended her indoor volleyball career, she has always suffered from problems with her knees—and there was a growing concern that she may require more surgery. But after working with our trainer, Phil, and some of the team doctors, she chose not to have surgery. She was beginning to athletes reach their goals. That means I have put my ego and personal preferences aside and do what's best for the team or the individual. After the barney in Switzerland I realised that I had to re-commit to my mission as coach—that's a lesson that came out of the Gstaad tournament. All the struggles we went through on tour gave us the opportunity to get together as a team, trust each other, and give it our all. I always tell Kerri and Nat that we do what we do because it's hard, not because it's easy. This was one of those hard times.

see that she had re-entered a good team, and that it wasn't my team; it was our team.

I trusted that when the time was right, everything would fall into place. As the saying goes: 'Let go and let God'. After struggling to convince Kerri of the value of Kurek's teachings, I eventually let go, and everything did fall into place. Kurek was around so often, and Steve and I had come so far, that Kerri felt a little obliged to participate. At first, she didn't take a whole lot of notice of me doing what must have seemed like crazy things. She thought I was just learning new life skills. But when it began to translate into performances on the sand she became seriously interested in teaming up with me again. After a while, she started going along to the meetings with Kurek and eventually worked with him on a one-on-one basis.

Our reunion wasn't without its initial hardships. Not long after we had regrouped, we almost fired Steve as our coach. We felt that he wasn't giving us what we needed. In Switzerland, after a ninth-place finish in the Gstaad tournament, we sat in the stands to discuss our performance. It ended in a fight. We were shouting; Steve was kicking chairs; everyone was watching. It was ugly. We decided we didn't want him as our coach any more. We were so close to the line, and so focused on our goal that we didn't realise how close we were. Steve was just pushing our buttons and we didn't like it.

There was still the burning desire to win. We knew we were close. In order for us to get back to our path, we had to respect each other; we had to regain the certainty and the team vision. I went back to that fundamental question: This is happening for a reason. How do we make it better? Once we decided to keep Steve on as coach, we began to realise that everything we had gone through with him could help us and make us stronger. If we wanted it to.

Now, back to firewalking. Kerri decided that she should do the firewalk. But even when she was standing in front of the fire, ready to do the walk for the TV cameras, she was saying "I don't have to do

" Control Your Destiny or
Someone Else Will "

Noel Tichy and Stratford Sherman

this!" Eventually we walked together over two lanes of fire, hand-in-hand, which meant that when one of us went, the other had to follow. We both had to be ready at any time. We had to be there for each other. Kerri got off the other end with tears in her eyes. Kerri is a champion and a very strong woman. I'd never seen her react like that. She said "I feel I can do anything now!" The fact that an accomplished athlete like Kerri could say that made a huge impression on me. I'd overcome my own barriers, but that doesn't mean I was in no need of reassurance.

Walking across glass was a different matter! I'd never been burned before, so walking on fire was something new to try. But Kurek had another trick up his sleeve. Everywhere he goes, Kurek carries with him, wrapped up in a sheet, a pile of the most frightening, jagged broken glass you have ever seen—made up of broken beer bottles and wine bottles. For effect, he tosses it on the ground as a joke and says, as the sound of smashing glass fills the place, "Careful, it's fragile". He then spreads it out and challenges people to walk on it.

One day, he spread the glass on his balcony and challenged me and Angela, who was still my partner at the time, to walk across it. To my surprise, Angela and Steve did it without hesitation. It seemed to be nothing for them. I was amazed and horrified. I had a real problem with this test and this fear was all about my history, again: I had cut my foot before. This was different to the

Kerri on the firewalk

When I met Kurek my reaction was "Well, he's a crazy bald American dude". I thought "If he wants me to do the crazy stuff he's doing with Nat, it's not on. I'm not really into that". I guess I didn't feel that my personality needed it. But he did change the way we worked as a team.

Before I did the firewalk, I thought that I would be totally open to it and take from it what I could. By the time I got to the other end I was extremely emotional. I felt awesome! It's not just walking across the coals, it's everything that is attached to it, including the way Kurek prepares you. After the walk I felt I understood what Nat had been through. I think that was the real benefit of the walk for me. You can compare the Olympics to that firewalk for Nat. She stood before the coals in Atlanta and was too scared to cross. In the years that followed she realised that it was her fear and self-doubt that was holding her back. At the Sydney Olympics she was a different person, a much stronger individual. And she's only going to get better.

firewalk. There was a script that I hadn't discarded, and it read like this: "When your skin comes into contact with jagged glass, you get cut". Who wouldn't believe that? It seems logical. To walk on glass, I needed trust. I needed blind faith, and I didn't have either. This is what I meant earlier about belief. It's not just a concept; it's something that has to be proven and practiced.

Kurek's point was this: you have a dream; you need to act as though you've already attained that dream. You need to be in your dream, as though it's real. He challenged me to come along for the ride, to step into that dream.. But to do that I needed to get rid of the last traces of fear and doubt, and the path would be so much easier to walk.

I stood there in the corner of his balcony, terrified. I hung onto the rail, tears streaming down my face and said "I'm not walking on that glass. You're all crazy! I'm going to cut my feet". Kurek responded with a question: "Do you trust me?" I said "Of course I trust you! But if you told me to jump over that balcony, I wouldn't do it. And I'm just not going to do this".

I don't know how he managed to persuade me. He asked me "What is it going to mean to you on the other side?" He knew that this was going to be a huge turning point for me, and after a while, he convinced me that it was imperative, absolutely essential, that I do it. My own fear was the precise reason that I needed to go through with it. That core belief I thought I'd been developing was nothing but fluff if I didn't attempt to walk on that glass. Somehow, he convinced me that there was no turning back.

I was scared. I broke into a sweat. The Voice was saying "You'll get cut, you'll get cut!" I tried to combat it by replying "I know, you idiot. But if I don't, I'll still

Take a leap of faith. Leave your comfort zone.

get cut somewhere in life". I was standing half-way up the mountain, and needed to make a decision. Step forward into growth, or back into mediocrity. I knew that on the other side was my budding belief in myself. When I let go of the side of that railing, I let go of my fears and doubts. When I walked across that glass, I was walking some of the final steps of my dream. Following the glass walk I knew there was no way that I was ever going to just have a dream without knowing quite what it meant or how I was going to get there. Kurek had laid a definite, deliberate path to the dream, and each step worked. After that, how could it not be achieved? The whole thing was beginning to make powerful sense. I realised that when I was just idly dreaming—hoping for the best, trying different things and 'failing'—I was proving to myself that my ambitions were beyond me. I hadn't really been serious about those dreams in the first place.

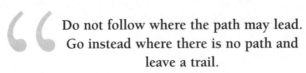

> **Do not follow where the path may lead.
> Go instead where there is no path and
> leave a trail.**
>
> *Ralph Waldo Emerson*

Kurek on my glass walk

I did not convince Nat to go. She made that decision herself. She was really scared about walking on broken glass because as a child she had been badly cut by glass on the beach. She was buying into the belief that her past is equal to her present. It is not. Every time you make a new decision, and take new action, you get a different result.

I asked Nat what fears were holding her back from the things she wanted. I asked her what she needed to let go of in order to reach her goals. The glass walk is all about having faith. Faith is the ability to see the invisible. I asked Nat "Who are you now and who will you be on the other side of the glass walk?" At that point I could see a change in her eyes. She knows that I would never put her in harm's way. When she decided to do the walk she developed trust and faith, in herself.

Her tears before the walk were fear and ego trying to stop her evolving. Her tears afterwards were about her purging the 'fear energy' out of her body. The whole experience was another level in her 'Jedi Knight training'.

I was beginning to understand what it meant to do things for myself. I had been aspiring to win an Olympic gold medal, believing that somehow I would find a way. But at the same time I was also closing doors, saying "I've done that and it didn't work"; or "I've tried to tell myself how good I am and it's pointless". I didn't have a structure, and I didn't have a teacher. To stay deliberately ignorant is to stay in your comfort zone. I was still comfortable believing negative things about myself, because it meant I would never have to take the risks necessary for success. Success is a risk because it means doing things that you've never done before. And, as Morpheus said in *The Matrix*, once you know, you can never go back.

The willingness to risk creates the opportunity for success.

Steve Anderson

Most people are completely unaware that they possess the courage to do the things they never thought possible. Why? Because if they were aware, they'd have to try it—and that's a risk. Most people play it safe. They are afraid of venturing into the unknown. The real reason most of us are afraid to make a commitment to excellence is our fear of failure. I lived with this fear of failure for many years. And to stay in my comfort zone I would sabotage my success. Sound familiar? Subconsciously we pull back when we get close to our goals—just *in case* you give it everything you've got and it doesn't work. At least then you can tell yourself later that you still had a little something left in reserve.

The tragedy of life is not that a man loses but that he almost wins.

Heywood Braun

Steve sat me down one day and asked me to ask myself how good I wanted to be. He said to really think about it. I have often asked myself this question. But this time was different. He made me seriously confront the question. Then he asked me if I wanted to be successful. "Of course", I would reply, puzzled. "Don't we all?" He proceeded to explain the secret to success in the following way.

- Success means different things to all of us, but I think it is fair to say that most of us do want to be successful, right? Do you really want to be successful? Are you willing to what is necessary to achieve your success?

- These are important questions because even though we want to be successful we don't always do the things that help us to achieve our goals. We want to, but sometimes—whether it is out of habit, fear of failure, fear of success, or just plain fear—we eventually do things that sabotage our own efforts to achieve our goals. We don't mean to and we don't consciously try to do it. It just happens.

- I believe that we all have a burning desire to be successful. But no matter how strong the desire, want and desire alone are not enough.

- I have no doubt that we all try our absolute best to achieve our goals. Trying your absolute best is not enough.

- Some of us go as far as to sacrifice our health, our happiness, and even our lives to accomplish our goals. I hate to be the one to tell you, but this too is not enough.

- You see, success comes at a high price. And it only comes to those who are willing to risk failure. Your success is directly proportional to the amount of risk you take. Are you willing to risk failure as much as you wish to succeed?

- Are you willing to be uncomfortable, to struggle, to compromise, to lead, to follow, to understand, to demand, and to sacrifice?

- You have to be willing to do things that don't come naturally to you. It is these things that keep you from achieving success.

- Don't get me wrong—you don't have to be miserable and forever wallowing in pain to accept the challenge of change. In fact stretching your comfort zone should be celebrated as a learning experience that enhances your life and moves you closer to what is most important to you: achieving your goals.

- We don't find it comfortable to stretch ourselves beyond what we know or to put ourselves in situations and circumstances that do not feel safe or secure. These are the places in which we discover new things about ourselves that help us conquer our limiting beliefs and the habits that lead to failure. It takes a willingness to do what is necessary in spite of what we feel is our nature.

- **Now, are you willing to do what is necessary to be successful?**

They say that "when the student is ready, the teacher will appear". Mine had appeared, because I was ready. I was ready to do what was necessary.

After Leanne, a very dear friend of mine, first introduced me to Kurek, a part of me said "You have to keep going with this guy". But there is a vast gap between desire to learn and the getting of wisdom. Wisdom will never come if all the lessons are easy. I also had to be ready to leave the comfort zone well and truly behind me.

After walking on glass, I asked myself "What does this mean to me?" It means that if you do all the preparation and learning and have the belief, then you will be taken care of. If you step with certainty, and don't panic, you'll be okay. If I hadn't panicked doing something I genuinely feared, something that I thought involved physical danger, then I wouldn't panic if Kerri and I found ourselves 11–8 down in the beach volleyball final of the Sydney Olympic Games.

In fact panic was nowhere to be seen in that match. There was no way I was going to panic. I was ready. I'd walked across fire and glass!

> **We must travel in the direction of our fear.**

Remember this

- Experience will tell us something is impossible. A seemingly impossible act—and plenty have been performed—has no precedent, so naturally experience will tell us it can't be done.
- One of the biggest barriers to success is to say "I haven't achieved it before".
- It's impossible to grow and stay in your comfort zone at the same time.
- New learning must be carried well. If we alienate others by being arrogant or bombastic, we've learned nothing!
- Are you willing to do what is necessary to achieve your goals.

Part 3

The winner is...Sydney

Source: AP/AAP

Chapter 16

Loving the struggle

Before embarking on our last world tour before the Sydney Olympics, we set three major goals. One was to win an event, to get that feeling of winning so that, as with the firewalk, we could tap back into that feeling: we would have a reference for the experience of winning. Two was to beat every team we may encounter at the Games, and there were only two that we hadn't beaten at one time or another. Three was to maintain a high standard the whole way, instead of winning one then coming fifth.

We managed to achieve two of these goals. What we didn't do was win a tournament. We beat all the teams we needed to beat: the Brazilians Adriana and Shelda, who we were pretty sure would make the final in Sydney; and America's Holly McPeak and Misty May, who we beat in the last game of the World Tour in Japan. Before this game against Holly and Misty, we played the semi-final against Adriana and Shelda and lost badly. We came off the court depressed, but Steve said to us "This happened for a reason, because now you have to play Holly and Misty, and they're the only team you have left to beat. So go out there and beat them". And we did, for the first time. It's amazing how you can always find a new perspective on all situations.

We realised we had beaten everyone we needed to beat: our self-belief was reinforced. We hadn't won a tournament, but the feeling of winning the ones we needed to win was very important to us. Most importantly, we played consistently to a high

Kerri on the breakthrough in the lead-up to Sydney

The breakthrough for the gold medal was when we finally managed to beat Adrianna and Shelda about two months before the Games. They beat us the weekend after that, but by that time knew we were capable of beating them. The following weekend we won a game against the American team of Holly and Misty, a team we hadn't yet beaten. These were turning points for us, because by the time we went to the Olympics there was no team we had not beaten at least once. This was particularly important given that we had not yet won a tournament.

While our we did not achieve our goal, in the lead-up to the Games, of winning an event, those two wins in themselves were crucial. They gave Nat and I strength of mind. This—combined with Kurek's work on our confidence, Phil's work on our bodies, Steve Anderson's belief in us, and our faith in the effectiveness of our preparation—was enough to get us to the Games with a winning attitude.

Despite the lack of tournament wins before Sydney, Steve reveals that we refused to be rattled. We stuck to our plans.

We were in a similar situation to the lead-up to the Atlanta Olympics. We had planned to win tournaments that would give us valuable experience. So for Sydney, I had marked particular wins as important for us to achieve. The basic plan was to have good finishes in the beginning of the tour, to peak somewhere around the middle—so that we would be making finals and winning events—and along the way to beat certain teams, thereby showing them that we had moved onto a new plateau. We needed to beat Adrianna and Shelda so that they would respond to us as champions. And the plan was that once we had shown them we could consistently beat them, then they would have to chase us, instead of vice versa. By the time the Olympics came around, we would have the edge on them.

standard. We were reaching the semi-finals on a consistent basis, finishing third three times and fourth once. In the games we lost, we played at a much higher standard than we had ever played before. We felt we could honestly say, without making excuses, that we weren't losing; at that point in time they were beating us. This was our time for learning. We were working on aspects of our game that needed fine-tuning, having narrowed them down to a few manageable things. As Bob Proctor said "There is a season to sow and a season to reap". This was our season to sow.

We accepted that we didn't just need to win; we needed to struggle; to fight the battle. In some of our games, we were going down 17–15, 16–14. But they were battles to the end, and we weren't spitting the dummy as we might have in the past. Importantly, we noticed we were slowly adding new weapons to our game all the time. And we were amazed at our own patience! We had certainly come a long way. A maturity to our game was beginning to show through.

 Adversity causes some men to break; others to break records.

William A. Ward

In Canada, we lost a match to Brazil, the World Champions, 15–8. They won but we left them with a warning: it was a titanic physical and psychological struggle. At the time I wrote "They won this time, but we know we are close. It's like a tidal wave building itself up from out at sea, and it's planning to crash on the shores of Bondi on September 25th. Lessons were learnt and battle lines drawn".

Chapter 17

Arrival

I mentioned earlier the importance of making space in your life for the things you want. On 20 August 2000, the mental space I had created came together with the real, physical space in which we were going to win the gold medal, and I took advantage of the experience to inspire me.

Ironically, Bondi played host to the largest beach event ever in Australia.

On that date I breathed, felt and relished the experience of being the first to step onto the sand inside the huge stadium at Bondi Beach. I didn't stand there wondering what might occur, what this stadium might hold for me. Internally I had already called it my own. Funnily

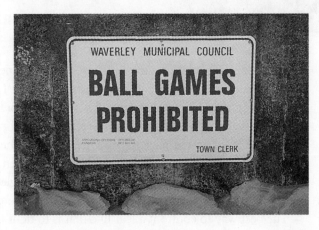

enough there was a voice pulling in the opposite direction, in the form of a sign that said, ironically, "Ball Games Prohibited". It could have served to reminded me of all the trouble the Olympic organisers had obtaining permission to erect the stadium, and all the protests from the locals, which were still occurring. But I decided to see the humour in it and laughed it off. Nothing was going to rob me of the power of that experience!

I stood in the middle of that stadium and in my mind I filled it with 10,000 Aussies, all cheering for Kerri and me. As I ran myself through that experience, my heart was in my throat and shivers went up and down my spine. It was an important thing for me to do, and it was one part of our preparation that would put me ahead of the opposition. I felt an overwhelming urge to feel a part of the stadium. I was soaking up the atmosphere and creating an image in my mind of

Claiming my territory

a full house. I was marking my territory. I asked some painters working on the site if I could have a go at painting the stands. I felt I could be at one with the stadium if I could help in some small way with its preparation.

The more I prepared myself for the experience of playing in front of a home crowd, the less I would have to worry about it on the day. I guess it's a bit like giving a speech. That's an experience that often terrifies people. Many concentrate on the contents of the speech and neglect to address the biggest issue of all: the fear of getting up in front of all those people.

The best way to confront a fear like that is to do it in calmer times, when the thing that's causing the fear is not actually physically present. You need to create the image of the crowd and imagine looking out at it. Run yourself through your movements and *mentally rehearse* things such as your attitude and approach. *Remind yourself to enjoy the experience. In other words, understand everything about your reactions* in advance and address them when there's no pressure. When you concentrate on those processes, you remove all those mental barriers that prevent you from employing your true skill.

> **Nothing in life is to be feared. It is only to be understood.**
>
> *Marie Curie*

Other experiences helped me to develop a mood for the Games. Running with the torch in Byron Bay surrounded by everyone I love and drinking in their support helped me to connect my experience with theirs, raise my own expectations of myself and convince myself that I wasn't going to let them down.

And then on 31 August, we arrived at what was to be our home for the forthcoming month in Sydney. It was at Randwick and initially there was some disappointment about not being at the village with the 'big' team. But we had to turn it to our advantage. The first thing Kerri and I did was to decorate the entire place with all the trappings of success and objects that inspired us. We hung a mock gold medal from the fire sprinkler on the ceiling and put Australian flags around the room. We also built a 'scoreboard' with our names on it and the score '15' under them, so we could always see ourselves reaching 15. On the walls was my Yoda poster, Michael Jordan poster,

A burning passion.
The final run for home!

There was no other option.

and a gold swimsuit. I put up pictures of the view from my home in Brisbane, and of the stadium at Bondi, right next to my bed. By the time we finished decorating, it was a golden shrine!

And of course, there were the gold volleyballs, gold shampoo, gold toothpaste and my gold camera! Now we could call it home.

There were plenty of reminders around that, at this stage, I was still a *bronze* medallist! On 3 September, we did an interview on Seven network's *Sportsworld* with Bruce McAvaney. The theme? Bronze medallists from Atlanta. Michelle Timms was the other guest and of course the topic was "Can they turn bronze into gold?" Michelle said that every athlete dreams about standing on top of the podium but while she was saying it I found myself thinking "A lot of people *do* dream, but dreaming on its own doesn't work. It's only the start. It's what you hold in

On your marks. Get set. GO.

your mind while you're transforming yourself and your life in order to attain it. I might be sitting here as a bronze medallist, because that's part of the game. But in my mind, I'm here celebrating my gold medal in advance!" I'd made all the choices (not sacrifices!) and done all the work that would lead only to gold.

Remember this

- No one ever became wise without struggle. Once you accept that fact, you develop a problem-solving attitude. Struggle is a vital learning experience.

- Surround yourself with the trappings of the success you've imagined for yourself.

- Use 'calmer' times to rehearse the way you will confront the things you fear. What will you do? What will your attitude be? What will the situation look like?

- When we go beyond dreaming, we can act as if we're already there.

- See yourself doing it. Feel the fear and do it anyway. Run through it over and over, so that when it happens you have been there so many times before that it almost feels like déjà vu.

Chapter 18

Busting out of doubt

The lead-up to Sydney certainly wasn't all smooth sailing. On 4 September I had a shocking time at practice. The sun was in the wrong place. The wind was swirling. I was getting frustrated and angry, and I was worried about my sore right knee. My legs felt sluggish. I knew I was being drawn into a downward spiral and, for a while there, there was no voice saying "STOP!" It seemed as though I had dug a hole for myself and, in a perverse kind of way, I wanted to see how deep I could go! It was as though, subconsciously, I needed one final test to see if all my learning really worked. I had to take myself to the darkest place and emerge from it on my own. But I was in danger of turning myself into a victim.

It happens to all of us. Negative emotions can become like friends. In order to keep them, we justify them by blaming external things. I was staying in the valley of excuses. If you're holding on to even one single negative emotion, it can cause you to spin your wheels and stay in exactly the same place for the rest of your life, if you want it to! And mostly, it has to do with blame.

So, of course, when Kerri and Steve offered advice, I didn't want to hear it. Steve reminded me that I needed to break the pattern; that external, physical things affect everybody, and that the main difference between competitors is the mind. "Forget how you feel and think now", he said. *The main thing is to make a decision: change.* Only by working on my attitude and revisiting my commitment to excellence could I reverse the cycle of negativity. So after being stubborn for a while, I came back to what I'd come to know best. Just as well I'd done all that practice! It was a bad time to revert to those old behaviours.

On 6 September, we had our media open day. It was to be the last time we were to speak to the media until after the tournament. Journos came from everywhere! I was really feeling the sense of occasion building, and it was exciting, and nerve-racking. I talked earlier about surrounding yourself with positive people. This was never more important to me than it was at that moment.

About three months before the Sydney Olympics, the organisers released the medals. A friend of mine, Danni Roche, a hockey gold medallist in Atlanta, rang me and left a message on my phone: "I've just seen the medals. They look great.

You'd better go and get yourself one". I now needed to harness all these positive voices. I didn't need people telling me how the Brazilians are the world champions and our job looked as if it was beyond us. We had people sticking microphones in our faces saying just that. In Atlanta I would have said "Well, they *are* pretty good. I guess we'll just try as hard as we can".

Now I had a filter system that turned my response into "Yes, the Brazilians are number one at the moment. And we will be number one next week". Only then could I respond to questions about them without becoming deflated. I answered: "Yes they are fantastic, and they've had a great build up. But our preparation's been good. We're ready for this". All we were really doing was acting like gold medallists, lifting our standard, and making ourselves accountable to thousands of other people. Inside we were thinking "Bloody hell! I have to do all this work; we have to win for all these people!" And that's where we wanted our thoughts to be.

> Our deepest fear is not that we are inadequate.
>
> Our deepest fear is that we are powerful beyond measure.
>
> It is our light, not our darkness, that most frightens us.
>
> We ask ourselves "who am I to be brilliant?"
>
> Actually, who are you not to be?
>
> You are a child of God.
>
> Your playing it small doesn't serve the world.
>
> There's nothing enlightened about shrinking so that other people won't feel insecure around you.
>
> We were born to make manifest the glory of God that is within us.
>
> It is not just in some of us; it's in everyone.
>
> And as we let our own light shine, we unconsciously give other people permission to do the same.
>
> As we are liberated from our own fear, our presence automatically liberates others."
>
> *Nelson Mandela*

We certainly weren't boasting, going around saying "We're gunna win". If we had done that, we would have learned nothing. The universe would somehow have taught us how to become gracious winners…and gracious losers! Besides, one out of every 10 of those little voices that we all carry inside us would answer back "Well, you haven't yet".

> **We are continually faced by great opportunities brilliantly disguised as insoluble problems.**

After our training sessions, Kerri was a little worried. As I said in an earlier chapter, training seemed so much easier. We were drained after training, but we were never tired. Understandably, Kerri thought we weren't working as hard as other teams were. I was a little more comfortable. I felt we may not have been working as hard *physically*, but we were working a lot harder *mentally and emotionally*.

Looking back on the four years—the training and the learning—and knowing our bigger picture, I was beginning to realise how right Steve was: it *is* all in the mind. There we were with gold medal aspirations, and not a win worth talking about. I guess everyone had a right to wonder how we were going to go against some of the best teams beach volleyball has seen in its short history. Throughout the lead-up to the games, when we kept losing semi-finals, people were saying "You've come third again (or fourth, or fifth). What happened? What went wrong?" But we got to the stage where we were taking Kurek's advice and celebrating our mistakes: our losses became mere stepping stones. We would reply "Nothing's gone wrong. It's perfect—right on target". Such doubt from others was understandable. All our friends were sharing our dreams but, of course, they weren't experiencing our journey. They'd come along with us and we were grateful for that, but we couldn't expect them to see the entire picture as we did—we were steeped in it.

I believe everything happens for a reason. As we lost each semi-final we were also working at getting emotional and mental stability and strength. If we had won all those semi-finals, we'd have got to the Olympics again and said "Well, we can do all this". Instead the semi-final become our most important hurdle and once we burst through that semi-final barrier, we knew we could do anything. It gave us a hunger.

Kerri on the lead-up to Sydney

Personally, I believe that I was not quite as fit as I had been in Atlanta, due to lots of problems with my knees. But working with our conditioning coach, Phil Moreland, we managed to overcome a lot of these problems and manage my knees by training smarter and not harder. We had also been through the whole process of preparing and playing an Olympic Games before, and no other team in Sydney had that. We were the only team still together, or together again, for both Games. This experience helped prepare us for the pressure.

About six months out from the Olympics I wrote this script for myself.

Because of time constraints, we didn't get to do all those things, but the whole script had been written, and my intention was to follow it as closely as I could.

The Script

September 15	Opening ceremony. March into Stadium Australia wearing the green and gold
September 16	Game 1 vs 24th seed
September 17–20	off
September 21	Game 2 vs 16th seed
September 23	Quarter final vs 8th seed and semi final vs 4th seed
September 25	GOLD! vs Adriana and Shelda at 2pm media drug test limo to Cathy Freeman's 400m final PARTY!

My Olympic script.

Chapter 19

Frustration

One week out from the Games, Steve, Phil, Kerri and I had a discussion about our motivation. Things didn't feel right. It's hard to explain, but we were so narrowly focussed on winning that we seemed to lack passion; we forgot to smell the roses. After all, we were in our home country and representing it at the Olympic games!

Time to relax and smell the roses with a SPEEDO beach day

Somehow, on top of all the other strategies for success that we'd been practicing, *we needed to renew ourselves*; to build on our foundations. Author Stephen Covey calls it "sharpening the saw". He believes that no matter how successful we become at reaching personal and professional goals, it can all come to nothing if we don't constantly renew ourselves.

I like the following quote from Cromwell: "He who stops being better stops being good". That says it all, and it probably explains something of where we were at the time. You can focus so hard on something that you become a 'closed system'. In other words, you forget about opening yourself up to all those other influences that you should be deliberately seeking; influences that help you to be better. Steve pointed out that the key was to have fun; to enjoy the entire experience of the Games, not just the anticipation of winning. Everybody needs reminding of that at some stage.

We were very fortunate in Sydney in that we had plenty of legends around us who wanted to help out with wisdom gained from their experience. So I was ready to receive the words of Peter Brock, who said "Love what you do, and stay focused". It was the first part of that equation we had to concentrate on. I made sure to order tickets to as many events as I possibly could. We also got into the Aussie mood of things as often as possible. There were the sing-alongs organised by the unique Laurie Lawrence, the barbeques, and a song called Rise, sung by Marcia Hines, that really vibrated with everything Kerri and I were thinking and feeling at the time.

Hush hush, opening ceremony uniform is a secret.

Thanks for the inspiration Marcia.

Steve on the team at the Olympics

It boiled down to maturity. We'd been there before, so we knew what the Olympics were about. We'd gone through a lot of transformations; Kerri and Nat had separated and come back together: they appreciated each other more and had become peers to a greater extent.

Kurek on the value of adversity

Anyone can steer a ship in calm seas. It takes a real champion to hang on when the ride is rough and you fear that you may not make it. If you let go when it's rough, you are guaranteed not to make it. Your only shot at success is to hang on and stay focused on your destination. Remember that your rewards are always in proportion to the test.

But I had a few other issues to overcome as well. With six days to go I still wasn't feeling great physically. I felt slow, uncoordinated, and my body hurt. I had failed to get opening-ceremony tickets for my family, so I was disappointed as I wanted my family to enjoy as much of the Games as possible. In fact, I had failed to get most of the tickets I had ordered. Phil organised for Steve to talk to me, and they reminded me of the importance of flexibility— the fact that champions rarely ever operate under perfect circumstances. Overcoming *imperfect* circumstances is what makes them champions in the first place. It was true, but took me a little while to digest it and get myself on track.

From the Sydney Diary, 9 September 2000:

Trust in the process and enjoy the challenge. In every moment be your best. Because that is your only moment—you will never get that moment back ever again.

 The ultimate measure of a man is not where he stands in moments of comfort and convenience, but where he stands at times of challenge and controversy.

Remember this

- Negative emotions can become our 'friends'. The only way out of it is to recognise the negative feelings we wallow in most frequently, and to consciously choose to say, or do, something positive in their place.

- The desire for self-renewal leads us to constantly examine and review our goals as our circumstances change. We need to ask "Am I on track?"

- Perfect circumstances never come. The key is to overcome imperfect circumstances.

- If we listen to people who have already been there and done that, we don't always have to learn from our own mistakes. They've been made before by others!

- Love what you do!

Chapter 20

The Games begin...again

We played our first game of the Sydney Olympic Beach Volleyball tournament the day after a stirring opening ceremony. Already we were surrounded by inspiration: five-time Olympian Andrew Gaze carrying the flag; Rachelle Hawkes reading the oath; the moving final lap that celebrated our greatest-ever female Olympic athletes; Cathy Freeman lighting the torch. And, of course, 110,000 jubilant Aussies in the stands. What a perfect time to achieve our goals, as long as the nerves could stay calm!

The next day, we watched the third-ranked team from America, Jenny Johnson-Jordan and Annette Davis, almost succumb to those nerves as they won a close match against our fellow-Aussies Sarah Straton and Annette Hygens-Tholen. Our first game was against Mexico. It was hard not to be overwhelmed by the crowd and the sheer sense of occasion. Our warm-up was very tense and shaky.

When our game began, the crowd made the whole experience an emotional roller coaster. Whenever we won a point, they went berserk. It was the highest we'd ever felt before. When we lost a point, the feeling of disappointment was tangible, and certainly audible! We felt as though we had just let everyone down. When the crowd let out a collective moan OOOOOOOHHHH— our spirits would dive. Ten thousand people would suck us down and it was so hard to get back up. Of course it wasn't their fault; they just badly wanted us to win.

Bondi stadium

Source: News Ltd

As a result, we began the tournament of our lives very tentatively. To be honest, we were intimidated. For a while the positive visualisation that I had done in the empty stadium seemed to come to nothing. In, say, Brazil, the crowd would cheer for us whenever we made a mistake. We dealt with this by putting up a wall. We never allowed ourselves to get too low. All we would hear was a solid wall of sound. But in Sydney, our wall was permeable. Familiar voices would get through. We would hear our names: "Kezza, Cookie, Nat, Potsy". It took some getting used to, but we knew it could only be a positive for us. We just had to make sure it was that way. We decided to relish the crowd; to *love* Bondi. It wasn't really that hard. It's just that the whole occasion took us by surprise.

We didn't play too badly in the match, but we failed to finish as strongly as we would have liked. In the end, we won 15–11. If we hadn't done so much mental training, we wouldn't have coped. We had made our own luck.

Time to fire up

The next day, our Aussie boys weren't so lucky. Lee and Julien lost 15–12 to Mexico, and we took particular notice of the way they handled the crowd. They too were tentative, and it showed in their setting and serving. They looked absolutely shattered. We decided there was no way we would go through that. Later, we went down to the stadium again to watch the Americans—Dain and Eric—and Aussies Matt and Josh play. This time, we wanted to soak it up, relish it, be part of the crowd; think the way they thought. They were unbelievable: electric, excited, constantly on the edges of their seats. By the end of it, all we wanted to do was get back out there and play. We had learned to love it! However, all the boys were by then in the loser's bracket, which means they had a hard road to hoe. We had to ensure that no matter what, our sympathy for them didn't translate into a negative mindset.

During our four days off, we identified the crowd as an issue. Yes, we'd learned to love all that microscopic attention, but we had never been there before. But there were other athletes around us who had experienced it many times; we just had to pluck up the courage to go and talk to them about it. We went into the Olympic village and spoke to Pat Rafter and Renee Stubbs, wanting to find out how they dealt with the hometown crowd. They were very forthcoming with advice. Pat went away and won the US Open twice, but when he comes home he struggles. At home Rafter gets "Aw, come on, Pat!" and that can be heavy stuff in the heat of a match. Pat told us he sometimes picks on the one Yankee in the crowd and just tells them to shut up. He tries to use it as motivation, to fire himself up. His advice was to generate anger if that's the emotion that helps.

Renee gave me some really valuable advice. She gave me a reason to smile in the final (you'll notice I did a lot of that). She said every time the crowd goes "OOOOOHHH!", it's all about changing your perception. What they're really saying is "OOOOOhhhh, we love you so much". They are telling you that they want you to win! So in the final against Brazil, whenever the crowd would do that, inside I'd be laughing, thinking of Renee's words. There's some truth in it. People in the crowd act disappointed because they do care whether you win or lose, not just for themselves, but for your sake, as well.

We also met with sports psychologist Phil Jauncey, and he reinforced Steve's words of positive *doing*. The tenor of his conversation with us was this: some people turn fear of a roller-coaster ride into excitement, while others stay terrified. Yet it's the same emotion. The difference is in the way it's translated. Regardless of what you think and feel, your muscles and neurones are still the same. The nervousness, fear and anger are okay to have, as long as you don't act on them. *Acknowledge they exist, and go out and do what you do anyway*. But keep it simple and *specific*. Focus on the things you do when you're in the zone. The muscle memory is there—I know how to focus on high/dynamic contact and hit the target, after all I had done it enough in practice. I just needed to release my mind and go for it. Most of the people we spoke to felt we would be better equipped in the next match—all we needed to do was to get used to the crowd and the feelings it generates. The faith of other people can be a powerful thing.

There are a multitude of ways to look any particular event. How many of you have reacted differently to the way your friends or family would in a given situation? Given a million dollars some of us will say "Beauty! I can have a house on the Gold Coast, a Lamborghini and the lifestyle I've always wanted". Others

Source: News Ltd

will say "Oh no! I will have to pay heaps of tax!" What we had to do was continue as we had been but see the crowd as an ally; see our opponents as smaller than us; see ourselves as gold medallists.

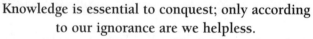

> **Knowledge is essential to conquest; only according to our ignorance are we helpless.**
>
> *Annie Besant*

Chapter 21

Inspiration

I'd come a long way since Atlanta, but I was still looking for inspiration all the time. Fortunately, there was no shortage of it in Sydney. The deeds of Kieren Perkins, Cathy Freeman, Susie O'Neill and Ian Thorpe featured prominently. I watched the swimming on a night when we got into three finals and won three medals. Susie O'Neill won the 200m freestyle, which wasn't even her pet event. I derived so much energy from participating in the crowd's celebrations that night. I loved all the hype, and just couldn't wait to get back out on the sand.

With Mum and Thorpe

By the time our second-round match came along—against China—we had learned a lot. Because of the four-day break, we were bored, excited, eager and restless. On the day, I couldn't stand waiting any longer (our game was at 5:15 p.m.) and headed to the Bondi stadium early to soak up more of the atmosphere and imagine myself out there against the Chinese.

When we finally got onto the court, we were a new team. We still had a few nerves as the crowd went ballistic, but we reminded ourselves that it was all about doing it anyway, nerves or no nerves. And we did it. Kerri's serve was right on the money and I felt I sided out well. We won the match 15–2. After the match, the crowd seemed totally obsessed—I felt like a rock star! It was a sensation I'll never forget. Dawn Fraser and I hugged. I asked her whether it gets better than this when you win gold. She smiled and said "It gets better! You'll be so high for the rest of your life, and you'll never come down".

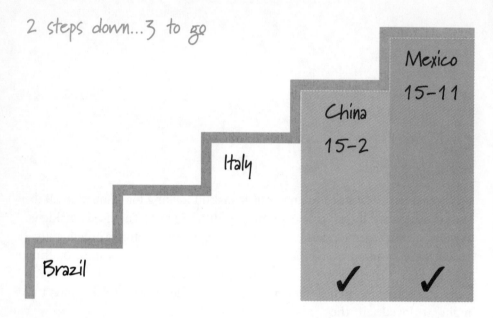

Sydney diary, 23 September 2000

2 steps down...3 to go

Brazil

Italy

China
15-2
✓

Mexico
15-11
✓

Kerri on the Sydney preliminaries

I think we became afraid of losing. We were certainly under extreme pressure to make the finals, and when we realised that we were just arms length away we let our concentration slip a little, made a couple of errors, stopped enjoying the game and got into that pattern of thinking more about trying to finish the game and worrying about it, rather than thinking about each point at a time.

23 September was the big day. We had two matches standing between us and the gold medal game, and they were to be held on the same day! We had to play like there was no tomorrow. We watched the Aussie team of Tania Gooley and Pauline Manser lose to Adriana and Shelda, the team from Brazil that we expected to play in the final. The Aussies finished the tournament in a creditable fifth place. Our favourite Yanks, Jenny and Annette, suffered a shock 15–9 loss to Japan. I think they will feel that loss for a long time to come.

Anna and Lara, our Italian opponents in the first match, were finely-tuned, but we started so strongly that we accelerated away from them to a 12–1 lead. We seemed to be doing *everything* right. They are a tough team, yet we were dominating them. Then something happened. It all went pear shaped. For some reason, we stopped and subconsciously questioned ourselves: why are we winning so easily? It was a real lesson, and I'm glad we learned it quickly before we lost the match. They fought back to 12–10, and showed us the extent to which volleyball is a game of momentum. We had that momentum going our way, and somehow we had forfeited it. As is typical with the game, the momentum then swung in their favour. In fact, it was more like an avalanche. We were suddenly struggling and had to quickly find a way to stop it. It caused a bit of panic in our ranks.

> **When I don't know whether to fight or not,
> I always fight.**
>
> *Nelson*

The Italians are a great team. They had no intention of giving in. We dug our heels in, maintained our belief, and weathered yet another a storm, one that we probably needed to have. We finally won 15–12, and were happy to wrap it up and get off the sand to re-group. It was good to learn the lesson against them, rather than against the Brazilians. From now on, we were going to finish strongly, and not give the opposition one inch.

We had to prepare for the next match. It was difficult to prepare mentally, because we didn't know who it would be. The Brazilian duo Sandra and Adriana ended up defeating the American team of Holly McPeak and Misty May—a minor upset. Then Adriana and Shelda, the other Brazilians, defeated Japan in the first semi.

Meanwhile, I raced back to the Swiss Grand Hotel, opposite the stadium on Bondi, to have Marcia fix up a few issues as well as receive some chiropractic work from Howard, another one of my saviours. I had built up our forthcoming match—the semi-final—to be *the* big hurdle. It was the equivalent of *that* match in Atlanta, and I had, spent much of the past four years working out what had gone wrong there. This was the bronze-medal match, and I had to get past it. Adriana Samuel, one half of our forthcoming opposition team, had faced us over the net that afternoon in Atlanta. The other member was Sandra Pires, who won gold in Atlanta. But how different Kerri and I were now! It was, in our minds, like a gold-medal match. We knew that if we got over this hurdle, we could do anything. Their team was made up of a silver medallist and a gold medallist. They'd experienced it all. They knew what it took to win.

When Marcia worked on me as we waited she helped me break down the final emotional hurdles I still had. It was a powerful, liberating feeling. While a few new butterflies were fluttering around in my stomach, I entered the stadium that afternoon determined and certain. Even writing about it now, my heart is racing. But I was happy with the nerves. I carried them without obsessing about them. As we came in, the roar from the crowd was deafening. We had never experienced anything like it, and we knew the Brazilians hadn't either!

Winners are grinners.

Steve on 'the zone'

After a winning game, when people ask you how you won, you often don't initially know how to answer. There's a thing called 'the zone' and the only way you can get into the zone is to free up your mind and let go of judgemental attitudes and all your thoughts. You have a quiet mind and you take that little voice in your head and you shut it up. You become hyper-aware. You can't go into the zone if you are worried or stressed or judgemental and that little voice is talking to you. The only way I know how to go there is by just expressing yourself and having fun. Look at the ball. Let everything go, and *play*.

In our minds, it was our moment. When we looked at them from the other side of the net, we said to them (in our heads) "There's no way you're going to deprive us of our dream. We want that gold medal. This time it's your turn". We again looked at them from the top down, not the bottom up, as it has proved to be such a powerful tool for us.

Sandra came out ablaze. She served the ball down Kerri's line. Ace. Down the middle of us. Ace. The next one was unreturnable. It hit the net, hit me on the shoulder and went out. Three–zero to them, after two minutes! I remember walking back to the reception position, looking down, then up to the heavens with a smile, and thinking "This is going to be a long day". That alone revealed something to me about the extent of my change. In Atlanta, I would have spiralled downward. I would have looked at the ground and not looked up again, and thought,

"There's no way we're going to win". In Sydney a 'long day' was nothing. It just meant that a long day was what it was going to take to win. This time, whether we were winning or losing, we had to act as though we were winning. Fake it until you make it.

How valuable now were the lessons I learned firewalking. Back then I stood in front of a path of fire and thought it would be impossible. Now I stood in front of the Brazilians and knew that it was not. The ability to tap back into that firewalking experience was the most valuable resource I had—I had experienced Natalie Cook doing something she thought was impossible. I now had a reference for that; a precedent that no one could take from me.

Kerri and I stuck to our game plan. Everything we did was directed towards finding a way to win and, what's more, we were enjoying the challenge. You could liken it to magic, akin to suddenly entering another dimension, but really it's just a coming together of attitude, preparation, poise and skill. Because we held our attitude, and never entertained the concept of losing—with all the emotional baggage that comes with it—we suddenly found ourselves in that dimension. It was a What is the Matrix?" experience. Suddenly we seemed to just be there, not because we sat back trying to comprehend it all, but because we kept seeing things a certain way, acting as though it was our reality. And so the reality in front of us fell away; changed into something else. Before we knew it we had won the match 15–6! We knew that our game was right where it needed to be.

With Monica Seles and Lindsay Davenport

Dawn Fraser capped it all off for us when she redefined the reality of the earlier match against Italy. She said that the reason fear crept in is that we had stopped enjoying ourselves. That made perfect sense. If anything is diametrically opposed to fun, it's got to be fear! What better way to block fear than to *replace it with fun*?

With family

Chapter 22

Golden Dawn

What was Dawn's advice worth? It was invaluable. We had done a lot of work in the last four years, but to be surrounded by so many wonderful people who wanted us to win and were prepared to unselfishly give so much of their time and advice was absolutely priceless. It's amazing how different, mentally, many of the great champions, or great achievers, are. They all have something valuable to say—even the quietest of them, if you press them.

This gives me something else to aspire to—not just their sporting achievements, but the great wisdom they've accumulated along the way, and the mentality that separates the best from the rest. More and more, I'm finding that this is the key to the attainment of anything in life.

 Great minds have purposes, others have wishes. Little minds are tamed and subdued by misfortune; but great minds rise above them.

Washington Irving

As I wrote earlier, there was no shortage of inspiration in Sydney. The day before our final, the Aussie water polo girls won gold over the Americans in the last hundredth of a second, with an inspiring goal from Yvette Higgins. The USA were probably 'supposed' to win that match. They thought the game would go into overtime (that's the power of assumptions), and then bang! All of a sudden the ball was in the back of their net! Our girls never ever gave up. It reinforced my thinking about self-belief. It was so good to see someone put it all into practice on the eve of the biggest game of my life.

When I awoke to 25 September, the day I'd been waiting for since 27 July 1996, I felt relaxed and focused. I believed in and valued the work I had done individually and with Kerri. There were no doubts, just some nerves and anxiety. This was our day and I had seen it unfold so many times that it was now a matter of enjoying the ride. In fact, I was so relaxed that before we entered the arena for

Steve Anderson on the blood, sweat and tears

Before we journeyed toward Olympic glory, I said that no one understands, and they never will, the sacrifices we have made, the determination we feel, and the bond we have forged. We fought hard against the whole world, Brazil and the US, and when all was said and done, we were one of the best. We celebrated, then we parted and went our separate ways, never to forget the path we had laid. And now we are united on that same familiar path to capture Olympic Gold and bring it home at last.

We be back. We be better. We be determined. We be together. With gold in our hands, gold round our necks, gold deep in our hearts. In every drop of our sweat: gold, gold, gold!

We've cried our tears. Now it is time to laugh, to grit our teeth and kick some ass!

Gold! gold! gold!

the final, I was on the phone to America —to a friend of mine, Liz Mazakayan. Liz didn't qualify for the 2000 Olympics (the second time in a row that she failed to qualify), yet she's one of the greatest beach volleyball players ever. I wanted to share this moment with someone who had been a great friend and a huge inspiration through all the lead-up. Before she snapped her kneecap in half prior to Atlanta, she was, with Karolyn Kirby, the world champion. The team split up then came back together for the Atlanta Olympic trials, but sadly she didn't make it. She was on the number one team in America six months before Sydney, but missed out again. I know how disappointing it was for her not to be able to represent her country in Sydney and wanted to allow her to share a small part of it.

Some people might think I was rubbing salt into her wounds, but I knew she wouldn't see it that way. I held out the phone and said "I'm in the stadium. We're about an hour away from the first whistle. Listen to this!" The crowd was deafening. They had just finished the bronze medal playoff, and 'Bondi Dave' (the Olympic beach volleyball MC) was geeing them up. I said to her "I'm about to get ready to play now, and I just wanted to share it with you. Can I call you after we win?" I stopped and realised what I had said. I didn't say, "If I win, can I call you?" I thought to myself "In my mind, I've already won". Of course I still had all the hard work in front of me, but I'd never been more ready for anything in my

> **The greater the obstacle the more glory in overcoming it.**
>
> *Moliere*

life. Before I went into the stadium I had made the decision that I was going to win. The most important work on my part was done: I'd made that decision, with no 'ifs' or 'buts'.

On paper, we probably weren't supposed to beat this Brazilian team. But nobody else had seen our piece of paper! Still, the comparative records were there for all to see. Them: 44 World Tour events, Goodwill Games champions (1998), World Champions (1999), 20 titles, 40 final-four appearances, 37 podium finishes. Us: 41 World Tour events, Atlanta bronze medallists, Silver medallist in World Championships (1996), one title, 11 final-four appearances, 9 podium finishes. By all accounts we should have been acting as if we faced an uphill battle. But we placed ourselves on top of the hill and prepared for a rapid descent—to victory. There was a calm silence between Kerri and me as we warmed up on the sand. We both seemed assured that no matter what happened, the other would put everything on the line. We also felt that we were not alone. Steve, Phil, Kurek, Kez and I were all out there together. The Dreamachine was one inseparable unit, and it was our combined efforts that had driven us this far.

I'm going to say something anti-climactic now. I can't remember much of the Olympic beach volleyball final. It was six months before I finally sat down and revisited the match on video. I want to hold it in my mind as something perfect—a new

level for us, which is really only a foundation for something even better! I knew that if I had watched it before then, I would have picked on every little thing that *wasn't* perfect. But I'll tell you some of the things I do remember, even to this day.

Before the match, Steve, our coach said two important things to us: "It might take a set; it might take a set and a half, but they'll start to feel the weight of Brazil on their shoulders and they'll crumble". That is precisely what happened. He also said "Everything you do out there is right".

At one stage in the first set, we were 11–8 down and all of a sudden we were serving for the first set. I remembered the water polo girls: never, ever give up! Back in Atlanta, which seemed not only another time but another dimension, I would have said "Oh well, it's 11–8, they'll get 12, we'll give them the first set, and start again with the second. Why waste energy?"

At 11–all, I stood back with the ball and kissed it. Then I said to myself "I may never get this opportunity again. If we lose this point, they could get the ball back, and they might win the first set". Talk about putting pressure on yourself! I told myself to go for it; take a risk. The willingness to risk is what creates the opportunity for success. Steve Anderson had drummed this into me for years, and it was at that moment that I truly understood its meaning. My serve hit the net. In any other situation in the past, that ball had always rolled back over to my side. This time, it dropped over their side! My Grandad died only weeks before the Games. Sometimes I like to think that he's the one who popped it over for us. That was a psychological turning point for us in the match. We knew that that it wouldn't matter if, in the second set, we were down again. We had no reason to fear or doubt.

I've got a picture of Susie O'Neill in my bedroom, with the caption: "Victory: when ten thousand hours of preparation meet with one moment of opportunity". The sentiment expressed in that poster really came alive for me at that moment. That's exactly what had happened. It was like a chemical reaction. The Brazilians started to make mistakes, and with every mistake they made we gathered momentum. We had built our emotional state to such an extent that when they challenged us, we braced ourselves and faced them head on. What's more, we enjoyed the challenge. Even when we missed the ball, we enjoyed the fact that we were in a fight. We weren't going to stop a great team—one of the greatest ever to play the game—from doing great things. Four years earlier, we would have been frustrated; we would have been upset about their points; we would have searched in vain for reasons.

Remember Dawn's words about enjoyment? It has often been said that we spent a lot of time smiling during that final. When we were beaten by balls, we were happy and excited about the challenge. I had come to the understanding that the way you interpret things affects your entire physiology.

> **There is no moment like the present.**
> *Maria Edgeworth*

Imagine there is a bank that credits your account each morning with $86,400. It carries over no balance from day to day. Every evening it deletes whatever part of the balance you failed to use during the day. What would you do? Draw out every cent, of course!!!

Each of us has such a bank. Its name is TIME. Every morning, it credits you with 86,400 seconds. Every night it writes off, as lost, whatever of this you have failed to invest to good purpose. It carries over no balance. It allows no overdraft. Each day opens a new account for you.

Each night it burns the remains of the day. If you fail to use the day's deposits, the loss is yours. There is no going back. There is no drawing against tomorrow.

You must live in the present on today's deposits. Invest it so as to get from it the utmost in health, happiness, and success! The clock is running. Make the most of each moment. There was one passage of play that people continually talk about. I mentioned it in the first section of this book, Bondi Gold. In the first set, I dug that ball. People are saying it will never, ever be dug again. One of the most famous beach volleyballers, Mike Dodd, was commentating, and he said it was

Steve reveals how that incredible dig was the psychological turning point in the gold medal match.

Nat's dig was an incredible play. I've never seen it done before in a match with that sort of pressure. It wasn't her ball and it really shouldn't have been dug, but you couldn't have told Nat that—she was so determined.

When the governing body of beach volleyball brought the 'let' rule in, I said "Ok, we'll practice this play". But it's so hard to practice for that. What we really did was cement the idea of never giving up until the play is dead. If you're truly out there to win, your one mission is to try to win until you don't have an opportunity any more. That's when the ball is dead or the final whistle has blown. Previously in practice, there had been times when we stopped trying once the ball hit the net. After the 'let'

rule came in we instituted a new rule at practice: if you made a play off the net during a rally, you got double points for it.

In fact, you can't practice for the play involved in Nat's dig. What you need is a mindset that you're going to go for it and win. That's what Nat's dig represented for me. It was a reflection of where she was at that moment. In fact earlier in the game the Brazilians had the same opportunity to dig one of Kerri's serves. If they had done so, it would have had a negative effect on us. When your opponent is making plays like that, and you're not making them, what does that do to your mental game? Thinking that your opponent is so committed and 'switched on' is intimidating. It's threatening.

"the single most extraordinary volleyball play" he'd ever seen. It was a ball that hit the net, and dribbled straight down toward the sand. Everyone in the stadium thought I wasn't going to get it. Later, when that serve of mine dribbled over the net, the Brazilians had the opportunity to do exactly the same thing, and Shelda had a reputation as one of the best "diggers" in the world. Same ball. I'd served it, it dribbled over the net, and Shelda just stood there. And that's how Kerri and I won the first set. The difference between the two sides, the difference between Sydney and Atlanta, the difference in my life, my outlook, my approach, was all in the mind, and it was the only difference that mattered.

A chance to thank everybody

The Dreamachine. We did it!

It's hard to explain how I felt when I dug that ball early in the match. Remember *The Matrix*? To dodge those bullets, Keanu Reeves's character, Neo, had to be in slow motion. I felt as though I was in slow motion that day. I felt as though I could have stood there for half an hour and I still would have got the ball. When friends ask about that moment I tell them to go and watch *The Matrix*. They usually come back and say "What the bloody hell are you talking about?" And I tell them to go and watch it again until they get it. It's easier than trying to explain it.

At that moment we knew, and the Brazilians knew, that the momentum was with us, no matter what the score was. The look on Shelda's face said it all. The Brazilians went out there with a fear of losing. How familiar it looked! It looked just like me, four years earlier. This time I was going to be the one taking advantage. So Kerri and I just kept chipping away at them. They led again early in the second set, but the rest of the match is a blur. The next thing I remember is the moment Adriana's final poke went out and the match—and the gold medal—was ours!

Kerri believes that the biggest difference between our bronze performance and our gold performance was self-perception.

In Atlanta we were tiny fish in a huge ocean. It was the first time beach volleyball had been an Olympic sport and the first time we had experienced an event of that calibre. In Sydney I felt like a shark in the ocean. I didn't quite feel like the biggest and most important fish, but I knew we were serious contenders with a great opportunity to be on top. And we were fighters: we went out there and attacked our opposition. We were on the offensive, there to get what we wanted rather than being bottom-feeders content with the scraps. In fact, given our attitude in Atlanta, it was a great achievement for us to get a bronze. By Sydney we had the valuable experience of an Olympics under our belt.

Kerri and I fell to the sand. Kerri was crying and repeating over and over "I can't believe it!" Every emotion I had felt over the last four years was condensed into that one moment. People have said that they can't believe how calm and controlled I seemed when I grabbed the microphone and spoke to the crowd. I wasn't that calm, believe me. I was excited. But I was also well rehearsed. The night before the final was the first time I hadn't dreamed and visualised volleyball for years. Instead, I'd dreamed and visualised that speech, word for word.

After all, Kurek had advised us to prepare for our new life beyond the gold medal. I dug my ditches in anticipation of the rain. Instead of sleeping I thought about how I was going to thank all the right people.

When I say we thought and believed we would win, I want to stress that this has nothing to do with being overconfident or arrogant. Winning was like déjà vu. It was all a game and we had played the game perfectly. Thanks to our preparation, every piece of the puzzle was in place that day. The last piece in the playing relationship between Kerri and me clicked into place in that game, and we were on exactly the same wavelength. Each of us knew what the other was thinking; we didn't have to use words. I stood on the dais, looked around, and thought "Yeah…this is exactly how I pictured it!"

Reflecting on things and trying to gain some wisdom from them I now realise that the Sydney experience told me just how much things had changed for me in four years, as a result of my efforts.

Kerri on the opposition

Over the last 3 years Adriana and Shelda have raised the bar in terms of level of the competition on the World Tour. They are one of the most skilled teams ever to play the sport. I feel very honoured to have been able to play them in the final of the Olympic Games and I truly understand the sorrow they must have felt in not achieving their dreams. But, they are human . . . and all humans are beatable! I'm sure they will want their revenge and I'm sure that many other teams that did not perform as well as they would have hoped will be out doing their best to knock us off our perch. So, I guess a new journey begins and we must start all over again.

With Mum and Dad

In Atlanta, most of our opponents served to me. In Sydney, in the lead up to the final, everybody served Kerri. It slowly just switched around. Towards the end of the tournament, our opponents were realising they couldn't win on Kerri either, so they reverted to trying to make me crack. But I was not the same as I was back in Atlanta. My heart and soul had bought into the experience, and nothing was going to stop me reaching my destiny. By the time the final came around, our opponents didn't know what to do. Frustratingly for them, they had to switch back and forth between tactics.

In this way our opponents conferred power on us. It was a powerful feeling to see them undecided as to what our weaknesses were. When they targeted Kerri I would think "That'll do you no good". When they directed their tactics back to me I was just as determined to make them pay for it by forcing them to serve Kerri again. This has been an aim of ours as a team for years; to keep our opponents guessing; to have them confused as to who to serve.

Kerri and I want the standard we set that day in Bondi to be our *minimum* standard from now on. We want to go further. That gold-medal performance was not the best we can ever produce. But at that moment, we sure felt the best we had ever felt! It's a magical day when a mission is accomplished.

After we won our Olympic Games gold medal, Steve said "Now it's about respect...

about moving from being champions to being legends. And the only way to do that is to be consistently excellent." These women have actually reshaped the way beach volleyball is played. Prior to the world championships in Brazil where we took the silver, we hadn't quite mastered the game and put it all together. One of the American players approached Nat and said "What in the hell are you doing with your game?" Volleyball has traditionally been a straight up and down ball-control game. And they were *tweaking* it. Then we started to get the results, and they started to believe in their game— there was a point where they wanted to give up on it. Now it's pretty common to see people running backplays and outplays and doing what we do. And I don't think the volleyball community has given them credit for introducing this.

Source: AP/AAP

With gold medals
at Stadium Australia

Remember this

- We can choose the way we react to an event.

- If you seek inspiration and advice from those who have already been where you are going, the territory becomes familiar and less scary.

- We all get frustrated when things aren't 'working' for us. But there's always something working, and there's always something to learn from it.

- Congratulate yourself, and give yourself credit for what you have done, even if it's only a small step.

- Ask: Am I moving away from the pain, or toward the pleasure? Try to spend your life moving toward what you want, not away from what you no longer want.

- 'Reframing' an event in our mind is a powerful tool. We can then make it mean something else; something more favourable.

- Never, ever give up! When in doubt, fight!

Chapter 23

Last words

> **Success should not leave you full, but hungry for more.**
> *Susie O'Neill*

So, what happens after you achieve your goal? Is that it? Success is often a turning point. We spend our whole lives chasing it, but what happens when we get there? It's high-maintenance. It needs constant nurturing. Perhaps at an even more intense level than before.

After winning the gold medal, I felt as though a magic 'golden' wand had been waved over me! It felt as if, from then on, I would be able to perform at that level without having to work too hard. But, of course, it wasn't long before the universe gave me a wake-up call.

After our win, Kerri and I sat down and began to map out our new journey: "Woo hoo, we won!, and it was the most fantastic feeling. Now how do we make it better? How do we move forward?" The challenge was to make that gold-medal game our minimum standard. Kurek calls it stacking: stacking the mentality and the belief on top of what you have already achieved.

Now, I walk onto a court with a new belief. I *am* a gold medallist, my game is much better without even trying. I've anchored something to it that is going to carry me through. I've now got plenty of positive experiences to which to anchor my game, among them are the song 'Rise'; the experience of being in 'the zone'; the words, encouragement and love of all the people who wanted me to win; the inspiring performances around us during 'the greatest Games of all'. I will always be able to conjure those feelings up when I need them.

And now doors are opening, I realise I can have it all, and so can you. It's all there, if you want it: cars, houses, business success, whatever you desire. We weren't put on this earth to be teased, or driven crazy by what other people have, and we don't have. It really can be all yours.

I have written this book because I believe that the hardship, fear, 'failure' and the fight to overcome these things have given me some wisdom. I'm not saying I'm a wise person. I'm saying I've gained some wisdom that I would like to share. It was fun seeking out knowledge from those who inspire me. I try to seek them out in person, or speak to them, and I try to do it by reading their thoughts in books.

While I can't guarantee that if you follow these strategies you will achieve your dreams, I can assure you that you will be granted an opportunity to succeed, the chance to win gold, Your gold! It is up to you to *make it happen*. The dream gives you a reason to jump out of bed each day. If you live with that passion you will find a way, or you will make one. Be sure to identify where it is you want to go, as this allows you to build the pathway. A lack of opportunity is merely a lack of direction. If you do not know where you are going, how are you going to know when you get there? Always remember that the pathway will remain. If you fall off, just dust yourself off and climb back on the path. There is no failure, only learning!

I hope this book makes your journey that little bit easier and more fruitful. The journey isn't necessarily easy, but enjoy the challenge anyway. Take Henry Van Dyke's advice and "Be glad of life because it gives you the chance to love and to work and to play and to look up at the stars". Reach for the stars. If you fall short you're still on top of the world!

Postscript

As the sun sets, the wind calms and the golden sand settles, I sit and replay those unforgettable events that took place in September during Sydney 2000.

Bondi is now restored to its beautiful old self and as the water laps onto the sands of gold the stadium is just a memory…I stand on the boardwalk overlooking the place where Kerri and I fell to the sand after our win, and I have to pinch myself to make sure it all really happened. On that day the Dreamachine created history. Australia's first ever beach-volleyball gold medal was won, and on our home shores.

Now, as I continue on my journey for Gold Medal Excellence, it is even more important for me to go on implementing the lessons that I have learnt over the last four years. Kerri and I are now 'the hunted'. Instead of looking back over our shoulders, we are going to make our own path, and leave a trail.

Kerri and I were anxious and nervous, yet also excited by our next encounter with the Brazilians, Adriana and Shelda. It was some six months later in Macau, off the coast of Hong Kong. It was a strange experience. As Kerri and I walked into the hotel with our heads high and shoulders back, we were conscious that we were Olympic champions. We were about to walk a new path. Our preparation for the event hadn't been ideal because our sponsorship and media commitments were significant. We were a little unsure of how we would fare. After all, there had been a lot of partying and resting going on, and not a lot of training. Yet we had a new level of belief ingrained in our hearts, minds and bodies.

When we stepped out onto the sand an overwhelming surge of power coursed through my body. Walking out onto the court, I had every reason to believe in myself. When I started competing four years ago I had to manufacture that belief—at that time I really didn't have many runs on the board. I had to fake it, till I made it. Anything is possible if you believe. Success will come to those who believe hardest in the power of their dreams and for the longest period of time. You just have to stick at it!

As we faced off against Adriana and Shelda in the final of our first world tour event since the Olympics, we had a sense of certainty and power. It exuded from every pore of our bodies. Again, it was an epic battle. And we made some plays that only gold medallists could make. We played error-free, confident volleyball, and were again the victors. As we stood on top of the podium singing Advance Australia fair, there wasn't quite the same feeling as Bondi, but it was definitely a feeling I could get used to. At that moment, we were again on top of the world!

Looking back on my journey over the last four years I can honestly say that it was golden. I have learned so much. The most satisfying part of it all has been seeing the dream come true. Best of luck on your journey. Always believe in the power of your dreams. May the force be with you.

Go for gold!

Natalie Cook

BONDI 2∞ GOLD

Toolbox

Goals are 'signposts' on life's journey. If you have decided on your goals, you need to become the right vehicle for the journey. Here are some tools to help you to build and maintain that vehicle—you!

Resources

1. access to famous, successful people through books, tapes, videos and seminars
2. encouraging voices
3. your own inner voice
4. friends with a success mentality
5. pens and paper (write your dreams down)
6. imagination.

Before you begin to build your vehicle, it's important to notice any signs that the vehicle needs some work:

- **Blame**. If you're in the habit of seeing yourself as a 'victim', then you convince yourself that mistakes are never really your own. You believe that your troubles are always someone else's fault. This puts vehicle maintenance out of your control.
- **Ego**. Stop and listen to yourself. If you say things like "I already know that", or "I've already tried that." and yet you are not succeeding, maybe your pride is a barrier to learning new things. Your vehicle will be constantly stalling.
- **Fear**. This comes out in many ways. You might never leave your comfort zone; you might always be anxious about things; you might be 'paralysed' and never act on things; you might be in denial about your problems, rather than addressing them. If your vehicle starts at all, it will go around in small circles.
- **Cynicism**. This is usually related to fear. If we stay cynical, we believe that no one will ever put it over us. We believe we always see things that others don't. Your vehicle will always be veering off into comfortable little cul-de-sacs.

If your vehicle has all of the above, it might need radical overhaul, perhaps with the help of a third party—a friend, professional help, or a diary in which you can reflect and record changes. The key is attitude. If you have the desire to get to your destination, you will.

The dream maker

Uses: to sharpen the focus of your vision for yourself in the future. Remember, those who don't have goals are destined to work for those who do.

How to use it:

1. Take a blank sheet of paper and a pen.

2. Write down all the areas of your life you would like to improve (as a guide, these might be: relationships, health and fitness, spirituality, knowledge).

3. Draw a circle and divide up these areas as slices of a pie.

4. Rate each one out of 10, according to its importance to you right now.

5. Ask yourself "If I was already a 10/10 for this area, what would it be like; what would I be doing?" This is your ideal scenario for each of these areas.

6. Write down all the details of that ideal scenario. Describe your life when you're there! When you've finished doing this for each area of your life, you have a total picture of your life as you want it to be.

7. Under each heading for these areas, write goals that will help you reach these ideals. Don't restrict yourself. They can be big or small goals. The only limitation is that the first goals you set need to be attainable. Every journey starts with one step!

8. Set a deadline, or action date, for each goal, and then little deadlines along the way.

9. Prepare a physical space for the things in your life that you really want, so you have a constant reminder. Your mind will work towards filling this space!

10. Live the dream. Fake it till you make it! Once you know what your ideal life is, act as though you're already living it. Hold yourself to that standard!

The almighty you!

Uses: to create your ideal world in your mind; to supplement the 'dream maker'. It's good to create pictures of an ideal world in great detail. But it's even better to imagine that you, and only you, can create this world. So, imagine yourself sitting on a throne above your world. You can have anything you desire with a snap of your fingers. Now, think of the aspects of your life that you brainstormed under the 'dream maker' tool. If you had the power to instantly make each of these areas of your life the best they could be, what would they be like?

Examples:

- **Intellectual**: I'd know everything about success in life, and I'd have wisdom.
- **Relationships**: I'd be charitable, tolerant and encouraging.
- **Job**: I'd do only those jobs that are meaningful to me.
- **Health and fitness**: I'd have my own home gym, get regular massages, and have the ability to listen to my body.

No matter what you do, do it with these goals in mind.

The fear buster

How to use it:

1. Choose a calm moment, and relax, perhaps with some inspiring music that has pleasant associations for you.

2. Choose a situation that you fear most. Let's say, for the sake of this exercise, that
it is making a speech (you can adapt the following to any situation).

3. Imagine someone who is very good at the very thing you fear (for example, they speak with precision and confidence; they use lots of humour; they're open and friendly and conversational).

4. Watch them from the audience and take note.

5. Now, imagine you're up there, looking though your own eyes, out at the audience—the person you admire is still speaking, and interacting with you—until you feel perfectly at home with their style.

6. It's your turn to speak. Picture yourself doing all the same things the person you admire did, and as they sit next to you, they smile and banter with you. Keep doing
it until it feels perfectly comfortable. Just when you feel great, 'anchor' the experience. That is, do something like looking at the ring on your finger or slapping your fist into your palm. Remember that anchor. The anchor might even be the very music you're listening to while you're doing this exercise.

7. The next time you need to give a speech, trigger those positive experiences by using your anchor. That is, look at the ring, or slap your fist into your palm just before you do it, or listen to that tune in your head. If you have practiced the situation enough in your mind, this anchor will immediately recapture the positive state that you created for yourself.

The control panel

Uses: for putting fears into perspective.

How to use it:

1. Again, imagine something, or someone, you fear and pick a calm, quiet place and time.

2. Ask yourself how you experience that fear. Is it primarily visual? Auditory (sound)? Do you touch it? Do you smell it? Do you feel it emotionally?

3. Play with the image as though it's on a TV screen and you're in charge of the knobs. Zoom out and make the thing or person you fear smaller. Turn them upside-down. Imagine them in their underwear. If it's a voice that haunts you constantly, make it sound like Daffy Duck or Groucho Marx. Play with its volume.

4. Practice doing this constantly.

5. The next time you face the thing/person you fear, imagine them this way. I did this when I was intimidated by the home crowd in Sydney. Every time they let out a disappointed "OOOOHHHH" when we missed a shot or lost a point, I'd imagine they were saying "OOOOH, we love you!" It's part of the reason I was smiling so much!

The habit switch

Uses: for breaking habits that prevent you getting to your destination, and replacing them with new ones.

How to use it:

1. Pick the habit you want to break. For the sake of this exercise, let's say it's smoking.

2. Think of your mind as a blank screen.

3. On that screen, put a picture up. Imagine a situation in which you are not a smoker. How would your life be better? Would you bound out of bed in the mornings and race off to play a game of tennis? Smell the flowers in your garden for the first time in years? What would you look like?

4. Hold it in your mind. Recreate all the sensations of fitness and health. Take note of your physical sensations, your emotions and your attitude.

5. Now, shrink that screen, so that it's in the bottom corner of your mind, and leave it there.

6. On the blank screen that's left behind, put another picture up. This time, picture the situations in which you most crave a cigarette, when you most have the desire to reach for one. Take note of your physical sensations, your emotions and your attitude.

7. As soon as that desire is at its height, imagine the picture at the bottom of the screen suddenly becoming larger and filling the screen, that is, the picture of you brimming with health.

8. Keep practicing this until it becomes a habit of mind.

9. The next time that familiar moment arrives when you most crave a cigarette, deliberately fill your mind with that picture. After a while, it will come of its own accord.

10. Once you've resolved to stop your habit, replace it with something else. Sometimes, the best way to eliminate a habit is to make sure it doesn't leave a void behind. I once knew someone who got down and did ten push-ups every time he got the desire for a cigarette. At first, it constantly reminded him of what he was missing out on, as he gasped for air! After a while, he just got fitter and stronger.

11. Practice your new habit for 21 days. Don't resolve to do it for the rest of your life, just 21 days. You'll find it's more attainable. Most things become habits after that period, if you do them every day. During that 21 days, keep your mind off what you don't want, and on what you do want.

Self-edit

Uses: to give yourself the feelings associated with experience of winning, even when you might not have actually experienced it.

How to use it:

1. Think of a situation in life where you could have reacted well, but didn't. It might be on the sports field, or it might be in a social situation.

2. Run yourself through the entire situation as it actually occurred, with the outcome that actually occurred.

3. Change it. Imagine you acted in the ideal way. Re-write the whole experience in your mind so you can visualise yourself reacting in an ideal way. Feel the sense of triumph! When you've reached that point, anchor it (see the 'Fear buster' for an explanation of the anchor).

4. Practice this repeatedly, with breaks to distract yourself between each time.

5. Next time you face this situation, remember your anchor, and re-live that 'experience' of winning that you have created.

Repeat, repeat, repeat!

Uses: to supplement 'The habit switch'

Our coach, Steve Anderson, says that repetition is the mother of skill. If a physical skill is only developed through repetition, then this is the same with mental and emotional skill.

How to use it:

1. Write down three good physical skills you've learned through repetition.

2. Now, write down three bad skills you've learned through repetition.

3. Note how good you can become, even at bad things, if you practice them enough!

4. Name three bad emotional/mental skills you've developed through practice.

5. Next to them, list what emotional/mental skills you will replace them with. These might be new ways of reacting to an irritation, for example.

6. Get up and do one of those things, now!

7. Set a date 21 days from now, and do it up until that date.

The right question
(or, redefining the problem)

How to use it:

1. Think about the most dominant problem in your life right now (for example, too much weight; too little money).

2. Ask yourself: "What are the main questions I ask myself in relation to this problem?" The question might be "Why am I fat?" or "Why do my children keep doing that?"

3. Change the question. A new question might be "How can I become healthy?" or "How can I reward my children when they do good things?"

4. Write the new questions down and watch how these new questions generate new answers. The answer to the questions above might become "Develop a healthy eating regime and forget diets" and "I can reward my children with this particular treat, and if I need to punish them, withdrawal of the reward might be punishment enough!"

5. Turn the new answers into goals, by asking, "How will I achieve this?"

6. Brainstorm as many goals as you can.

7. Put them in order of possibility—which goals are more 'do-able' now?

8. Add them to your list of goals.

The power centre

1. Draw a scale, like this: M——————————E. This scale is the extent to which you are controlled by yourself (M) or by external things (E).

2. Put an X along the scale. If it's closer to E than M, this means that other people/things control your life more than you do. This leads to anxiety, stress and depression. And, of course, it means you're moving toward someone else's goals, not your own.

3. Identify what thoughts you have that take power over your life away from you. Categorise them. For example: blame—Who or what do I blame for failure or stress?; prejudice—What assumptions and dislikes prevent me from acting in positive ways; fears—What fears prevent me from acting? conditions—what external conditions prevent me reaching my goals? (for example, lack of money, dead-end job, and so on). You might be able to think of more headings.

4. Prioritise your top three in each category, and resolve to work on just these, with patience, and perseverance!

5. Now, write down those areas of your life in which you have most control, and associate with the most satisfaction.

6. Think of ways to work on these strengths and enhance them. For example, think of areas of your life to which you've never applied these strengths. What changes can you make that bring your life into closer alignment with the things you want, the things that empower you? An example might be to have more contact with successful people.

Remember that using these tools takes mental discipline, but it begins with a desire to change. If your desire is strong, you will follow these steps in great detail. You will find that you move toward your thoughts. Our nervous system doesn't know the difference between a real event and one that is created by our mind. So take control of your mind!

Appendices

World Tour results

Date	Event	Country	Nat's partner	Result
2000	Osaka (Japan)	JPN	Pottharst	3
2000	Espinho (Portugal)	POR	Pottharst	3
2000	Toronto (Canada)	CAN	Pottharst	3
2000	Marseille (France)	FRA	Pottharst	4
2000	Berlin (Germany)	GER	Pottharst	5
2000	Chicago (USA)	USA	Pottharst	5
2000	Rosarito (Mexico)	MEX	Pottharst	5
2000	Chicago (USA)	USA	Pottharst	5
2000	Vitoria (Brazil)	BRA	Pottharst	7
2000	Gstaad (Switzerland)	SUI	Pottharst	9
1999	Osaka (Japan)	JPN	Pottharst	2
1999	Espinho (Portugal)	POR	Pottharst	2
1999	Acapulco (Mexico)	MEX	Clarke	3
1999	Dalian (China)	CHN	Pottharst	5
1999	Toronto (Canada)	CAN	Clarke	7
1999	Salvador de Bahia (Brazil)	BRA	Pottharst	9
1999	Marseille (France)	FRA	Clarke	9

1998	Salvador	BRA	Clarke	5
1998	Espinho	POR	Fenwick	5
1998	Rio de Janeiro	BRA	Clarke	5
1998	Vasto	ITA	Fenwick	7
1998	Toronto	CAN	Fenwick	9
1998	Dalian	CHN	Clarke	13
1998	Osaka	JPN	Clarke	13
1998	Marseille	FRA	Fenwick	17
1997	Pusan	KOR	Pottharst	3
1997	Marseille	FRA	Pottharst	4
1997	Pescara	ITA	Pottharst	5
1997	Osaka	JPN	Pottharst	5
1997	Melbourne Women's Open	AUS	Pottharst	7
1997	Rio de Janeiro	BRA	Pottharst	7
1997	UCLA Los Angeles	USA	Pottharst	9
1997	Espinho	POR	Pottharst	9
1997	Salvador	BRA	Clarke	13
1996	Osaka	JPN	Pottharst	1
1996	Atlanta Olympics	USA	Pottharst	3

Dreams do come true

The Sydney 2000 Preliminaries

15 September:
Opening ceremony

16 September:
Round 1 vs Gaxiola and Galindo,
Mexico, 15–11, 41 mins

21 September:
Round 2 vs Xiong and Chi,
China, 15–2, 30 mins

23 September:
Quarter final vs Bruschini and Solazzi,
Italy, 15–11, 39 mins

23 September,
Semi-final vs Pires and Samuel,
Brasil, 15–6, 36 mins

25 September, Final vs Bede and Behar,
Brasil, 12–11, 12–10, 115 mins

1 October: Closing ceremony

Source: AP/AAP
(and photo on p. 143)

We all have a dream. Deep down inside the flame is burning brightly, and sometimes its light comes to the surface. But you push it back because you think you can't do it…The truth is you can! You just don't know how to achieve it.
Find a way…and then make it happen.

Dream your own dream

Dream your own dream
And follow your own star.
There wouldn't be a heaven full of stars
If we were all meant
To wish on the same one.
There will always be dreams
Grander or humbler than your own,
But there will never be a dream
Exactly like your own,
For you are unique
And more wondrous than you know!
Do your best.
There are no shortcuts
On the way to a dream,
So give all that you have
To all that you do.
And above all things,
Believe in yourself.
This is all your dream asks of you,
But this is everything.
Linda Staten

Suggested reading

Lessons from the Art of Juggling, Tony Buzan and Michael J. Gelb

Chicken Soup for the Soul [all of them!], Jack Canfield and Mark Victor Hanson (Health Communications)

Dare to Win, Jack Canfield and Mark Victor Hanson (1996 Berkeley Publishing Group)

Don't Sweat the Small Stuff (and it's all small stuff), Richard Carlson (2001 Hodder Headline)

You Can Be Happy No Matter What, Richard Carlson (1997 New World Library)

How to Stop Worrying and Start Living, Dale Carnegie (1948 Simon & Schuster)

How to Win Friends and Influence People, Dale Carnegie (1989 Angus & Robertson)

The Way of the Wizard, Deepak Chopra (1996 Harmony Books)

Child of Dawn, Gautama Chopra

The Richest Man in Babylon, George Clason (1991 Penguin)

The Pilgrimage, Paul Coelho (1992 HarperCollins)

The Alchemist, Paul Coelho (1995 Harper Perennial)

The Valkyries, Paul Coelho (1995 HarperCollins)

7 Habits of Highly Effective People, Stephen Covey (1989 Simon & Schuster)

Get Up and Go, Lisa Curry (1988 Harper Sports)

The Transformed Mind, Dalai Lama

The Art of Happiness, Dalai Lama (1998 Hodder Headline)

Body, Mind and Sport, John Douillard (2001 Three River Press)

You'll See it When you Believe it, Wayne Dyer (1990 Schwartz Publishing)

The Sky is the Limit, Wayne Dyer

Manifest Your Destiny, Wayne Dyer (1997 HarperCollins)

A Good Walk Spoiled, John Feinstein

The Edge, Howard E. Ferguson

Fast Track to Success, Jane Flemming (2000 Penguin)

The Inner Game of Tennis, Timothy Gallwey (1974 Random House)

Sheer Will, Michael Groom (1997 Random House)

Go for the Goal, Mia Hamm (2000 HarperCollins)

Winning Attitudes, Ian Heads and Geoff Armstrong (eds) (2000 Hardie Grant)

The Ultimate Secret to Getting Absolutely Everything You Want, Mike Hernacki (1998 Berkeley Publishing)

Think and Grow Rich, Napoleon Hill (1966 Hawthorn Books)

Success Through a Positive Mental Attitude, Napoleon Hill and W. Clement Stone (1989 Angus & Robertson)

Sportsmind, Jeffrey Hodges (1993 Hawk Personal Excellence Publications)

Kieren Perkins, (1997 Pan Macmillan)

Greg Norman, (1999 Pan Macmillan)

Sacred Hoops, Phil Jackson (1996 Hyperion)

Feel the Fear and Do it Anyway, Susan Jeffers (1992 Fawcett Books)

Slaying the Dragon, Michael Johnson (1996 Hodder & Stoughton)

I Can't Accept Not Trying, Michael Jordan, Sandro Miller and Mark Vancil

For the Love of the Game, Michael Jordan (edited by Mark Vancil) (1998 Viking)

Into Thin Air: A Personal Account of the Mt Everest Disaster, Jon Krakauer

Rich Dad Poor Dad, Robert T. Kiyosaki (2000 Warner Books)

Lawrence of Australia, Laurie Lawrence (1993 Ironbark Press)

Five Ring Fever, Laurie Lawrence (2000 L. Lawrence)

Get Motivated: Daily Psych-ups, Kara Leverte and Shelia M. Curry (1994 Simon & Schuster)

The Game of Life, Karen Levin (1998 Pan Macmillan)

The Warrior Within: The Philosophies of Bruce Lee to Better Understand the World Around You and Achieve a Rewarding Life, John Little and Linda Lee (1996 Contemporary Books)

Running with the Bulls, Luc Longley (1996 Ironbark)

Michael Jordan Speaks, Janet Lowe (2001 John Wiley & Sons)

Winning, Michael Lynberg

The Greatest Salesman in the World, O.G. Mandino (1982 Bantam Books)

Lion Heart, Jesse Martin (2000 Allen & Unwin)

Life 101 [series], Peter McWilliams (1994 Prelude Press)

Way of the Peaceful Warrior, Dan Millman (2000 H.J. Kramer)

The Inner Athlete, Dan Millman

The Sacred Journey of the Peaceful Warrior, Dan Millman (1991 H.J. Kramer)

Body Mind Mastery: Creating Success in Sport and Life, Dan Millman (1999 New World Library)

Be Positive, Harry Mills [quotable gems] (1993 Business Library)

Anatomy of the Spirit, Caroline Myss (1997 Three River Press)

Changing Habits, Changing Lives, Cyndi O'Meara (2000 Penguin)

Choose to Win, Susie O'Neill with Fiona Chappell (1999 Macmillan)

Road Less Travelled, Dr Scott Peck (1997 Simon & Schuster)

Further Along the Road Less Travelled, Dr Scott Peck (1997 Touchstone Books)

The Celestine Prophecy, James Redfield (1995 Bantam)

The Tenth Insight: Holding the Vision, James Redfield (1996 Bantam)

King of the World, David Remnick (1998 Random House)

Awaken the Giant Within, Anthony Robbins (1993 Fireside Books)

Monica, Monica Seles

Think Like a Champion: Building Success One Victory at a Time, Mike Shanahan (2000 HarperCollins)

Tiger Woods: The Making of a Champion, Sports Illustrated

Zen Mind Beginners Mind, Schunryu Suzuki

Bruce Lee Fighting Spirit, Bruce Thomas (1994 Frog Ltd)

The Atlanta Experience: An Inside View, various (including commentaries by Bruce McAvaney) (1996 Harper Sports)

Half Empty Half Full, Susan Vaughan (2000 Harcourt)

Conversations With God: An Uncommon Dialogue, Neale Donald Walsch (1996 Hodder Headline)

Completely Calm, Paul Wilson (1998 Penguin)

Internet resources

Our goals could not have been achieved without a very special team around us. Below are some of our team, new and old, who I am sure would love to help you out. Please don't hesitate to contact them, and tell 'em I sent you!

- **Kurek Ashley**. Kurek needs no introduction. www.kurekashley.com

- **Marcia Pitman**. Marcia is able to de-sensitise people to their allergies so that they can, on occasions, eat foods to which they were previously allergic or intolerant. Marcia is also very good at changing people's perceptions, as part of their total well being. She uses a process that deals with emotional factors blocking (sabotaging) a person's capacity to function effectively in certain situations. It restores confidence and competence in situations in which people might otherwise have been overcome with fear, anxiety or feelings of inadequacy. www.lifeworkshealthclinic.com.au

- **Fit 2 Peform personal training**. Headed by Jeff Wagstaff, Fit 2 Perform develops your body, mind and soul so you can perform to the best of your ability. Fit 2 Perform has developed a dynamic and innovative approach to fitness training that allow you to achieve your goals. Get Fit 2 Perform...in all areas of your life! www.fit2perform.com.au

- **Peter Spann at Freeman Fox**. Freeman Fox provides wealth-creation education and services for independent investors who seek financial freedom. Ranging from seminars that teach people how to invest and the most profitable strategies to follow, to financial planning, investment advice, property, shares and finance. Peter's seminars also include personal development sections. He is a must see. Contact Freeman Fox on 1800 000 369 or visit the website at www.freemanfox.com.au

- **International Quarterback**. Chris White and his team manage our affairs off the court. www.iqsport.com.au

And be sure to follow our new journey on the websites www.beachvolleyball.com.au **and** www.nataliecook.com